LIONHEART

The name given to one battle tested by fate when he lives life displaying, Resilience, Fortitude, Perseverance and Ambition

Copyright © 2014 Rayshawn L. Wilson
www.RiseandRoar.com

ISBN-13: 978-0-9827-6321

Published in the US by Legendary Publishing Company

Front Cover Design- Marshall Shorts
Back/Side Cover Design- Marshall Shorts, Stefani Qamil
Wright

Editors
Andre Lampkins
Melissa L Webb
Stefani Qamil Wright

LIONHEART:

COMING FROM WHERE I'M FROM

RAYSHAWN L. WILSON

I say what others will not. I do what others will not. I AM who others will not be. I AM limitless, boundless, infinite, and measureless. I AM the Roar of Truth because I CHOOSE to be!

INTRODUCTION

There was a point in my life when the path I traveled was a source of shame for me and a constant reminder of a hurtful past that I wished I could just move beyond. Then there were moments where because of how far I had come, my journey served as a source of pride. Over the years I've sat on occasion and retraced my steps with close friends and loved ones, and each time I did I felt a bit more liberated.

I also remembered one of the seven principles of the Nguzo Saba that I learned about in college. The principle of Kujichagulia, Self-Determination, says that we should define ourselves, name ourselves, create for ourselves, and speak for ourselves. It was with those thoughts that I even entertained the idea of telling my story. Once the idea became a final decision, there were a few causes that fueled my motivation:

• Most often we learn of African-American men making the news after committing a crime and becoming a part of the criminal justice system, resulting in a representation in the media as discussed.

• As consumers of mainstream media, we hardly ever hear, see, or read about individuals who part company with the criminal justice system and actually go on to make something of their lives, negate the statistics of recidivism, or better still, contribute to society in meaningful ways.

•Thousands of children are placed in group homes, foster homes, and other institutions every day. Their stories, whether of doom and failure, or resilience and achievement, are non- existent.

For those of us who have triumphed over the adversity of the foster care and criminal justice systems, we have put ourselves in an elite class. I don't use the word elite because we are better than those who fail or struggle. I use the word elite because it takes a special person to rise in the midst of being weighed down by so many forces that we often had no control over. This will be a sharing of my pain, my joy, my deepest inner thoughts, and the plan that God had for me long before I knew who He was.

Throughout each chapter, God's grace, mercy, and countless blessings will be put on display and hopefully reaffirm for some and confirm for others that He is indeed in control. As I type, and as you read, there is a child who has just been placed in a foster home, or just witnessed one of his parents being taken to jail. There is also the young man who is explaining his innocence to a public defender, or a parent who just smoked crack cocaine instead of providing food and clothes for their child.

I feel an obligation to all four and then some, including my own children, and I've been able to realize a certain level of success that makes it imperative for me to share my story. I do not seek exaltation in relaying my story, but I hope to lift others up and eventually liberate them from their own struggles. Standing on the shoulders of countless unnamed and unknown men and women who fought and died for what they believed in gets a little unstable when the wind blows, but the fear of losing my balance never stopped me from standing.

A long time ago, I committed to facing the wind and rising no matter the trial, no matter the weight. Because I'm not the first person to rise, I knew that it could be done and because I'm still rising, I know how it feels. So whether the words within this book reach one person, a few people, or a few thousand, I believe that I've done one of the many things God has placed me here to do in writing this book and doing so with passion and purpose.

Simply put, I hope the pages of this book help to demonstrate that it is not what you go through, but how you come through that matters the most. Failure only becomes a reality once it is accepted.

Jeremiah 29:11 says, "For I know the plans I have for you, plans to prosper you, and not to harm you, plans to give you hope and a future." The numbers of this verse happen to be my birthday, and I'm telling you God never makes mistakes. My experience constantly teaches me that God doesn't make mistakes no matter how painful it may be in the beginning.

If you have ever been in prison, group homes, foster homes, hurt by loved ones, felt a sense of abandonment by loved ones, been unable to forgive, struggled with addiction, or just need some motivation to press forward in life, then this book is for you. I've started to create LionHearts all the across the world. Each one of you that reads this book will see a characteristic of yourself as a LionHeart, which embodies traits like ambition, perseverance, fortitude, resilience, and faith. The time is now. Not tomorrow, not next week, not next month, it is time right now to Rise & Roar!

"To love an addict is to run out of tears"
~Author Unknown

CRACK COCAINE

My life has often been examined with bended lenses, which only result in circus mirror-like distortion. In this game of life we are all forced to play, but I have always felt like nothing was ever set up with me to be the benefactor, the hero or triumphant in the end. In school I learned about Sisyphus, who was a character in Greek mythology. In his story, Sisyphus was forced to forever roll a rock uphill only to watch it roll back down. I sometimes envied Sisyphus because I was forced to chase a rock that was constantly rolling downhill. It appeared that I would never be on the side of the rock that would allow me to push it up the hill.

I'd watch how other kids lived, how other families functioned, and how other parents interacted with their children and it became clear to me that I was ill equipped to participate in the game, and unaware of the rules by which everyone else was playing. Based on what I know now, not only was I unaware and lacking the tools, but I was without the necessary coaches. I endured childhood during the crack cocaine pandemic. To put it plainly, crack cocaine was as deadly as anthrax, and the police evoked the same kind of terror as an Al-Qaeda suicide bomber. Crime was as constant as breathing and provided more promise than tomorrow.

No other narcotic known to man has had the ability to devastate, kill, separate, and destroy in the African American community way that crack cocaine has. The devastation I speak of began at my own home, as my mother became addicted to the drug. My childhood began in sunny California and contrary to popular belief, everything in California was not sunny.

Some of my most vivid memories of a childhood that was filled with adult situations involve the realization that my mother had a substance abuse problem. I was raised to know my place as a child and that meant I was helpless in addressing a problem that would lead to years and years of hardship, anguish, and heartache. My rock continued rolling downhill. Denial became a familiar friend and it was the way I dealt with the hurtful realization that I was becoming a victim of crack cocaine. I continued to rely on denial to be there in the way that some youth would rely on a parent to help with homework, and he became a faithful friend until we moved to the south side of Columbus, Ohio.

Maybe denial was opposed to cross-country moves because he sure didn't make the trip with me. The Lincoln Park housing projects were known as "Skid Row", and its name preceded it. The drug activity, crime, low self-esteem, and sense of helplessness were higher than I ever experienced and worse than I could have ever imagined. In the same way that the cover of a book is supposed to grab its reader and indicate what is to be found within, the entrance into the projects provided its own indication.

The long one-way street seemed to be dark and gloomy no matter the time of day, and the exit that leads out was no different. Options only came if you were familiar enough with the side streets and back alleys to navigate your way through them and find a way out, but those options were littered with potential pitfalls and dangers of their own. After living down off skid row for about six months, I was still waiting for my buddy denial to show up and he failed me in a major way when a classmate forced me to deal with my mother's addiction. We were on the basketball court and his words still cut like a knife, "Hey Shawn, I just saw yo mom comin' out the crack spot around the corner. Man wassup wit that?"

The shock, hurt, and embarrassment I felt were insurmountable. Just as I thought of ways to deal with him and save face, my friend finally showed up. Denial, where have you been? I simply replied to the boy, "Man you must have the wrong person." The kind of exposure I had avoided with my old friend's arrival saved me from constant ridicule and victimization. The truth was, and still is, that there were more parents smoking crack than will ever admit it, but once a person was addicted it took control of their lives and nothing else mattered. Not their children, not losing their jobs, not finances, not laws, nothing.

Once a kid's mom or dad was labeled a crackhead, there were no limits to the ridicule, and to allow myself to be ridiculed would make me look weak, and among the first things I learned while chasing my rock downhill was to never look weak. Weakness, or the perception of weakness, opened up the door for so many other problems. I knew it was my mother leaving the house where she went to cop drugs, but I was not about to look weak.

Shortly after that day on the basketball court, I began to notice more and more traffic coming in and out of my mother's apartment at all times of the night. Our door was open more than it was closed, and I could tell by the level of the draft if the door was open long enough to let someone in, or if they walked in and left it open. When silence settled in, I knew it was only because my mother was outside on the block with the folks that she smoked with and copped from. I would know that for sure because I could see it all unfold from my bedroom window.

The end of the month came and brought with it more opportunities for my mother to feed her addiction. The remaining balance of her food stamps was sold for half price in exchange for cash, and the cash was used to buy crack. I'm thankful that my mother would feed me before feeding her habit, proving that she did in fact love me. I just wished she would have loved me enough to completely kick the habit. During our stay in Lincoln Park projects, I learned that many of the small time drug dealers were kids who were my age or slightly older.

With that being the case, I also went to school with many of them. As a youngster I was always pretty observant and understood the concept of action and reaction. Even at school I had to deal with the evidence that my mother was smoking crack. Those same young guys that she bought her drugs from were the same guys at school who had the Air Jordan sneakers, Damaged jeans, gold Gucci link chains, and *Starter* jackets. And there I was with the Charity Newsises winter coat, and plastic sneakers from Picway. A great deal of hurt came from knowing that my mother's addiction financed their wardrobes.

At times, my mother was masterful at balancing her addiction with motherhood, and then there were times when I would wonder if all hope was gone. When we found ourselves out of food or money, my mother would either sell crack for the local drug dealers for a small kickback, or she would sell dummy rocks (fake drugs) to strangers and make sure she was long gone before they realized they had just bought a fake piece of crack. My mother's apartment was close to the alley, which was considered the hub of all of the activity and ideal for the dealers when they needed to take cover, or use a stove to cook up a new batch.

I can remember knowing how to cook up a batch of crack after only watching a couple of times. Watching this step-by-step process was like watching a mad scientist conduct an experiment. I became all too familiar with the distinctive odor of crack and whether it was being cooked or smoked, I would always know when it was time to go outside. Ironically, sending me outside was my mother's attempt at shielding me from the activity that was taking place while the outside was no different.

The one thing that going outside did allow me to do was have an opportunity to spend more time outside than I would under normal circumstances. What this meant for me during adolescence was that I would get to go to the mall on a shopping trip furnished by my mother, or go to the skating rink. She seemed to be extra nice during these times and would hand me as much as a hundred dollars and her only instructions were, "Don't spend it all in one place."

Many times I would go buy clothes or other things that would make me feel like a normal kid. What I didn't spend I learned I would have to hide in order to keep. My bedroom became the first stop along the journey to scrounge up money once mom had spent all of hers. I remember having to resort to hiding my money in my underwear because I knew that was the one place that was off limits. My mother tried her best to keep the drugs and the activities that seemed to be the focal point of her social life away from me, but her addiction coupled with the environment we lived in would have it otherwise.

On the day that denial left for good, I can remember walking cautiously up the stairs to peek around the corner into her room. Before my eyes I was witnessing my mother smoke crack. I had actually caught her in the act. I sat on the edge of the step and watched her methodically put the piece of crack on the pipe, stick it in her mouth, and light the fire. As the crack burned, it began to sizzle and pop. She inhaled slowly and blew the thick white smoke into the air even slower.

She repeated the lighting process several times, and each time the cracking and sizzling sound would get more faint than the time before, until finally it was gone. With the last cloud of smoke from her mouth came a thought, "That fifty dollars sure did burn fast." That could have easily been food in our cupboards, a bill paid, or some better clothes for my younger brother and me. Instead of sneaking back downstairs, as loud as I could I jumped up and yelled, "Hey! Whatcha doing?!!"

From my experience with those whose drug of choice was crack cocaine, I learned very quickly that being scared, startled, or snuck up on wasn't anywhere on their list of favorite things. Not only did she damn near have a heart attack, but she also dropped her pipe, which broke. Once she realized that it was me, oh she was pissed that I had scared the shit outta her, and I was lucky to escape that moment in life without an ass kicking. Instead of allowing me to mess up her high she yelled, "What the hell you doing inside this house? Go play somewhere and shut my damn door!" I laughed so hard my stomach began to ache and I could hardly wait to slam the room door shut and avoid inhaling any of the smoke that still filled the air. To this day, I don't know how I was able to find humor in a moment that in hindsight angers me so much. Maybe laughter was replacing denial.

Unfortunately, that wouldn't be the last time that I would sneak up and catch her in the act. There came a certain level of innovation and ingenuity with being addicted to crack. I witnessed a number of different everyday instruments being transformed into crack pipes:

pop cans, car or television antennas, glass pipes stuffed with steel wool, and even aluminum foil rolled up and bent into the shape of a pipe.

Living in the projects, I witnessed the dope game up close and personal. My experiences allow me to recall drug deals, violence, and crime with specificity that at times begs the question, how am I here to tell this story? The answer is an ever-changing one, but one that always involves me acknowledging the grace and mercy of God. My bedroom window was like a picture tube into the reality of life in the projects because from it, I could tell you who was holding what, how much it would cost you, and who was a particular customer's dealer of choice.

The summertime brought out the best of the worst, and I would regularly see the dope boys standing on the block waiting for customers to walk or drive up. One of the things that surprised me was the lack of consistency in the folks who would drive into the projects to buy crack. A crack addict could only be picked out if they had a serious addiction. The other surprise came when there would be so many dealers standing on one block that it was fascinating to watch a car roll up and see people scurry and rush the car to get their sell off first. Dealers would ask how much they were trying to spend, and then pull out their biggest rock in that price category. It was almost like an auction where the largest piece won.

Sometimes customers would only buy from certain dealers due to trust. There were also those who feared buying dummy rocks. Then there were some dealers who managed to be well enough chemists to cook up the crack just right. They had what customers would say was the best crack on the block. This crack was not overcooked and wasn't diluted by too much baking soda. There were even times when the dealers would rush cars and hold their hand inside the cars in order to show their products only to have the potential customer smack their hand, causing the crack to fall inside the car. I saw a couple of these brave customers get away with ripping off the dealers, but the game changed once the dealers decided that they wouldn't take those kinds of losses.

Most of the time if gunshots were audible from my window, it was because a dealer was shooting at the car of a customer who tried to rob them. Under any other circumstances and in any other housing project around the country, this may not be strikingly odd but there is one factor that I have yet to mention. The Columbus Police Department had a police substation on the perimeter of the projects, and it was also visible from my other window in the apartment.

The police clearly knew of the activity and every once in a while there would be a few arrests, a raid, or a roundup which would get the current folks off the block long enough to make room for a new group of dealers. It was almost like they were being allowed to push their product long enough to be considered serious criminals, make some money, fall in love with the lifestyle, get locked up then released to spend the rest of their lives dealing with the criminal justice system, and trying to find ways to recreate the fast money lifestyle that crack created for them. The vicious cycle would repeat itself, for them and for me.

Over the years I watched the way my mother's addiction to crack cocaine completely took control of her life. The residual effects made it so that crack cocaine also had an immeasurable impact on my life and that of my brother. Most times I watched my mother work very hard to provide for us, but once crack took over, she would work hard for two weeks and smoke up all of her earnings during the weekends. So not only was there a shortage of money in our household, but there was a shortage of all of the things that money was supposed to buy.

Frequenting local food pantries became a normal part of our weekly grind in order to eat, and even that wasn't enough for two growing boys. Walking with our backs against mom in the supermarket allowed me to steal packages of meat and beans, items that she said, "Would stick to us," until our next meal. I developed a "gift" for stealing groceries from the local stores by creating compartments in my clothes, especially my coat in the wintertime. At 12-years-old I was a small boy and often looked over because of my size, so it was often easy to slip past people without being noticed. Many times I would return to the store two or three times to get what I needed, or to ensure I had a full meal to bring home.

I became very creative and out of necessity, I would use other shoppers to help me make it out of the stores undetected. While on one particular shopping trip, I packed my coat with food and I approached an elderly woman. As she was pushing her cart after checking out, I offered to help her push her cart to her car and load her groceries. The appearance I wanted to convey was that I was with this particular nice old lady and couldn't possibly be stealing.

Once that worked, I had a normal operation whenever I needed to go shopping for a meal. No storeowner ever suspected that I was robbing him or her several times a month. I got so good at it that I started to steal from stores because of the thrill and teenage desires, not out of necessity. There was a certain thrill and rush involved with not getting caught and being calculated. I had gone from feeding a need, to feeding a habit. I had a different technique for every store and devised different methods of stealing based on the store, the item, the flow of traffic, and even the time of day.

As it does with every criminal however, my luck ran out. I was at a grocery store near my mother's apartment when the manager on duty caught me. He grabbed me by my ear and pulled me all the way out of the door. Once he got me outside, he removed the shrink wrapped T-bone steak and the bag of frozen shrimp from under my clothes, and with a firm index finger cautioned me to never return again. Many of the habits I developed and learned as a young child were born out of necessity and came from watching and listening to my mom. They were meant to be survival skills, but the world where they were considered to be desirable skills is the world that was created solely by crack cocaine.

There were times during the month where Mom would call nearby fast food restaurants posing as a caseworker from the Salvation Army. She would get the manager on the phone and would go into a compelling story stating that she had a family who was recently burned out of their home and she was wondering if they could feed a family of five for one night. After playing on the emotion of the store manager, he or she would almost always agree. She would state that she was sending the oldest son to the restaurant to pick up the food and for that day, we would eat like normal kids.

The food was hot and fulfilling, but it was hard to be in the moment and enjoy. My belly was full, but I would get hungry just thinking about where the next meal would come from. Over the course of several years, she had to have called over twenty restaurants and all the while using the same name and variations of same story: Mrs. Williams, a caseworker from the Salvation Army attempting to help a family that was suffering due to unfortunate circumstances. The managers who came to know the woman who called occasionally had to admire a woman who was so connected to the community and went out of her way to make sure that a family in need had something as simple as a hot meal.

What most would discard after its shelf life expired meant the difference between burgers and fries or sleep for dinner. While addiction brings out the worst in people, I also know that it shows some skills that exist that are hidden by fear and lack of opportunity. Often times those skills are revealed when options are few and life's circumstances seem to be worse than the days before. If those skills were applied to life before addiction, I wonder if more people would be in a position to live on their feet as opposed to their knees.

Addiction prohibited any semblance of stability at home. Days, nights, and every minute in between were filled with uncertainty and dreadful anxiety that couldn't be expressed. Bending or creating our own truth was so much a part of the fabric that was our home life that the concept of real truth was nonexistent, as long as we benefited from the lie. Lying and stealing became as natural as breathing, and they were among the learned tools that were necessary to preserve life. Although my mother was imperfect and I knew enough about her actions to be disappointed and saddened, she was still my mother and I loved her.

My greatest fear at the time was that I would lose her to the effects of the dope game, and that fear was almost realized. The July day was so hot it sizzled like the crack I remembered hearing burn months earlier in my mother's room. The heat of the day didn't stop the traffic from backing up outside my window. In fact there was so much traffic, a passerby might confuse the pulling up and driving off with the lunch rush at a restaurant's drive through window.

The only difference was that there was no window and the hand to hands happened much faster. I sat and watched out of my bedroom window until the sun started to leave and taking the heat with it. As the cool of the summer night sky fell, the foot traffic began to build and the flash of brake lights illuminated my bedroom walls. The block began to bustle, so I wasn't surprised that my mother was an actor in this scene. Her set prop was the lawn chair that she dragged behind her until she got to her sitting spot, but I could never make out her lines from my seat in the balcony that was my bedroom window. The appearance of a large U-Haul truck struck me as odd.

I saw cars drive up that needed to be pushed away, and even cars so fancy and new that I had only seen them on television, but never a moving truck. The big box truck pulled into the alley and was then followed by two yellow cabs with black tinted windows. What I saw approaching from across the field on the other side of my periphery made me feel like my bladder was about to empty. Fear and panic caused me to try to yell out but I couldn't. By the time I was able to yell "Mom," several men dressed in all black with army-style machine guns drawn ran towards the gathered crowd.

In the blink of an eye, the back of the U-Haul truck came alive with several men jumping from the back dressed in the same all black and with the same guns. While all of the actors ran and scattered, I heard gunshots in the distance followed by FREEZE, DON'T MOVE, and FIVE-OH! The SWAT team came from every possible direction. I focused my eyes on my mother as she attempted to get up from her chair, but before she could stand fully erect, a cop put the barrel of his rifle a few inches from my mother's head and yelled for her to lie on the ground and put her face in the dirt.

I was downstairs with my hand on the latch of our screen door in what felt like one long stride down the stairs. Just as I opened the door, I was instructed to get my ass back in the house and not to come out. I had no choice but to watch the rest of the act from my bedroom window. Several arrests were made that night, but my mother wasn't one of them. The same misfortune that her addiction produced was the only reason she didn't have any drugs in her possession that evening: she didn't have any money. She couldn't concoct a story for any of the fellas on the block that would lead to a free rock, this want McDonald's.

She was held for a few moments, had a quick warrant check done and released. This was just one of many instances where SWAT would pounce on the projects, kick in doors, pull people from their homes, and drive off with someone's mother or father. The soundtrack to those scenes would always consist of a loud boom when the door was kicked or rammed, screaming and yelling, and almost all the time a baby or woman crying. With each raid, the police grew more creative with their approaches and disguises.

Over the course of my window watching and living in Lincoln Park, I saw police pose as UPS drivers dressed in all brown, construction workers with hardhats and jeans, and even as the ice cream truck driver with the music to match. None of these raids stopped the dealers or crowds that would gather, or my mother from going right back out there and doing the same things over and over again. Nor did it stop the addicts from coming back to cop. I would even see times when they would wait about an hour after a raid and set up shop again.

There was never a shortage of folks driving up to feed the monkey that lived on their backs. The allure of the high for addicts and the allure of the money for dealers were one in the same. One group was chasing the feeling of that first hit while the other was in pursuit of the almighty dollar. One group ended up with a temporary escape from reality that resulted in a return to a reality that was becoming a nightmare, and the other pursued easy money that would never be enough but would lead to costing things that money couldn't buy or fix. Both needed to realize that the highest peak, whether smoking or selling, could only be reached once and then you have to come down. It was like they were on a hamster wheel, both running but going nowhere.

Over the years, my mother's addiction and our instability worsened. The rent was always late if paid at all, so we pin balled from place to place, which meant different schools, different neighborhoods, and different places to go hustle up a meal. It never meant a fresh start. By the time it was all said and done, I had attended three elementary schools and four middle schools. It seemed that it didn't matter what type of neighborhood we lived in because in all fairness, there were some neighborhoods that were pretty nice, but somehow drugs and the lifestyle always found its way back into our home.

There were times when I could tell my mom wanted to quit, she just didn't know how. She was helpless against her disease. Once I overheard a phone conversation with a friend that she smoked with where my mother shared that she was trying to get her life together and spend more time with her kids. Hearing that conversation gave me hope that somehow things would turn around and life would be something closer to what I knew it should be.

Soon after that conversation I stood in my mother's doorway as she lay on her bed sobbing uncontrollably. As I stood quietly, she knelt and began asking God to forgive her, and to help her change her ways. I too said a prayer that day, but I didn't think He heard me. There were plenty of moments of clarity like that one, but the power of her addiction always overtook the desire to change, and it would be days, sometimes hours, before she would be using again.

In between our moves from apartment to apartment, we would sometimes find ourselves homeless. Mom once sold all of our furniture when we were living in the projects for cash. The story was that we were moving back to California, but that was a lie, as she had no intentions of moving us back. If someone had ever commented on how nice the furniture was, they were the first people to be offered an opportunity to purchase it. Needless to say, the majority of the money that came from selling our furniture was used to buy drugs.

Not soon after the furniture, all of our belongings were also being sold. So there we were with no money, no personal possessions, no furniture, and no place to go. The same Salvation Army that my mother claimed to work for during our hunger hustles was the same place that provided a temporary roof over our heads. Once we had exhausted the thirty-day period that we were allowed to stay at the homeless shelter, we moved back into another apartment.

Again, new look, new place, new belongings, but the same old problems persisted. Addiction kicked into high gear when Mom would disappear for days at a time, leaving me at home to take care of myself and my brother if he weren't dumped off at a relative's house. I had many lonely, tear filled nights. With no food, no mom in sight, and no desire to hustle up or steal a meal, sleep was my only escape. Some days I would restlessly roam the streets visiting old neighborhoods and seeing old friends. I quickly found out that some of those old friends weren't playing one-on-one basketball and had little interest in the things that we did during earlier times.

Many I found were caught up in the dope game as young as thirteen-years-old. Others weren't really selling drugs, but earned money holding drugs for the dealers and running errands in the neighborhood. The dealers knew that they decreased the risk of being caught with a juvenile holding onto the drugs, and even if the young children were caught, it was a quick booking process and release to the parents. In most cases, the youth mules were out the next day and right back to work.

The young boys were paid anywhere from one hundred to three hundred dollars per day for taking chances on ending up in the penitentiary. The jobs seemed easy enough, stand around and hold the dope until potential customers would approach, wait for a signal to produce a certain amount, and hand it off as instructed. Considering all that I was experiencing and all that I had lost with no indication that things would get any better, I was drawn to the jobs that so many of my friends talked about.

The idea of having that much money of my own meant that I could buy my own food, and more importantly, stop wearing clothes that made me the object of ridicule. The idea that I could buy my own name brand gear felt like instant power, no more helplessness. I grew tired and frustrated with other kids talking about me, or always having to go to charity or Goodwill to get many of my clothes. I didn't want any more handouts, especially if they were going to contribute to laughs, jokes, and embarrassment. Money became the great equalizer in the neighborhoods I lived in.

After being fed up with the ridicule, I understood why the guys in Lincoln Park stood around and risked being locked up to earn money. Along with the money came a sense of power, which produced respect and a lifestyle that on the surface was something I longed for. I dreamed and fantasized about money the way most teenaged boys dream about a girl. I wanted to hold her; I wanted her to be mine, to belong to me, and for others to see me with her. For as much as I had hoped and wished that things would get better with my mom, they never did, and as I got older, it was more difficult for her to hide her addiction. She could no longer just send me outside to play.

At thirteen-years-old, I had witnessed and experienced more real life drama and disaster than some watch on television, and more than most will encounter in a lifetime. Firsthand experiences contributed to me knowing more about the dope game and the ways of the streets than I knew about reading, writing, and arithmetic. My patience started to be wear thin with mom's addiction because quite frankly, I was tired of suffering because she wanted to get high.

The times when dealers would show up at our home to collect a debt of my mother's began to be more than I could count. All hours of the night they would show up with one hand extended and the other on their weapon. The game was changing because now she was getting crack on credit and these cats did not mess around when it came to collecting. When she wasn't able to pay up in cash, they often left with some household item under their arms.

I would press my ear to my bedroom door to listen to the conversation after hiding anything of mine that might even appear to have some monetary value. I began to resent my mother and I stopped being willing to try and understand her addiction. I stopped having hope that she would try to get better. I stopped believing that her prayers would be answered and as a result, I started being disrespectful and rebellious. When things didn't go my way, I would run away from home.

Most times I'd stay at a friend's house until I wore out my welcome, and then return home. Upon my return, I would stand in front of my mom and tell her how I hated living there, and how I hated her for making us live like that. As an adult, I've come to know that my hatred wasn't for my mother or the type of home that she provided. My misplaced hatred was for the addiction that ruled her life and tormented mine. During those short-lived stints as a runaway, I would fantasize about a better life. Not a perfect one, but one where crack cocaine was something we heard about on the news, and where I knew just as much in the classroom as I did on the streets.

I wondered what it would look like, what it would feel like to not be embarrassed by who I had to be, by who my mother was, by how we had to live. The days would come and go and I'd vacillate between hope and despair, but I always wished it would be better. The best days were ones where my mom was her real self, and wasn't high. There were many of those. My mother was very outgoing and fun-loving. She had a great sense of humor and could easily have me rolling on the floor in fits of laughter.

That's the woman who would show up in my fantasies and occasionally in real life to let me know that she was still hiding in there inside her addiction. She took great pride in her culinary skills, for she was an artist in the kitchen. Occasional Sunday dinners consisted of fried chicken, homemade macaroni and cheese, collard greens, cornbread, and German chocolate cake was her desert specialty. That was hands down my favorite meal of all time. Mom would always tell me that a good meal could change a person's mood regardless of what the trouble was.

To this day I stand by that and on those Sundays, that meal would provide the escape from my reality and the laughter would replace disdain. My mother was easy to love. No one knocked on the door to collect. I enjoyed a meal that didn't result from a lie or thievery, and the only smell in the air was that of the chocolate cake baking in the oven. On those Sundays my belly was full, as was my heart. I wasn't hungry, nor did I worry where the next meal would come from.

In the struggle for survival, the fittest win out at the expense of their rivals because they succeed in adapting themselves best to their environment
~Charles Darwin

ONCE UPON A TIME IN THE PROJECTS

To date, some of the best lessons life has ever taught me came my way during the 1980s and early '90s while living in one of the roughest housing projects in the city of Columbus. Seeing a group of boys my age playing tackle football in the field across the street from my mom's apartment is among the first memories. Climbing down out of the U-Haul truck, I instantly wanted to play. My mom was against it for a number of reasons: "Rayshawn, how about getting moved in first? Besides, you don't know any of those boys, how do you know they want you playing?"

Against her advice, I ran across the street to get a closer look at the action. Growing up in the late '80s, we seldom played organized football with teams because that was too easy. At least that's the way it seemed to us. The reality is equipment and all of the things that came with organized football came at a pretty expensive cost. Real men during that era played "smear the queer"; however, the use of the word "queer" had no connection to being gay.

It was simply the designation of the person who would be "it". The kid who had the football was "queer", and the rest of the kids, usually about 10-15 of them with no age or weight limits, would chase the "it" kid down until he was tackled to the ground. Those that were hard to take down usually paid the price because you would often have multiple kids hanging all over your body trying to drag you down, or you would have people coming from all different directions trying to take your head off.

It was contact football without the luxury of having any teammates if you were the running back. Once the "it" kid was tackled, he would launch the ball high in the air to wait and see who the next brave kid would be to pick up the football and attempt to score. If you were brave enough to touch that ball, you had better be running as soon as you took possession. The more kids that played the game, the harder it was to score a touchdown, and the more likely you were to get hurt or injured.

Many kids lost teeth, suffered from concussions, and regularly had the wind or shit knocked out of them. There was a big advantage to being quick on the pickup so as to get a better running start. No one kept score and no one wins. The game was a modern day gauntlet and rite of passage that every boy played in neighborhoods like mine. To us, it was a game that tested our courage, allowed us to practice some athleticism, to blow off steam, and release some aggression. The glory came to those who would earn a good reputation in the projects for their courage to pick up the ball no matter who was around, their ability to elude would be tacklers, and finally score.

My first night in Lincoln Park I learned a few hard lessons that still resonate today. After darting across the street I stood watching the game from the sidelines. I sized up the field from end zone to end zone, and even pictured myself taking the ball and running the distance. A few minutes of watching and analyzing the field, the players, the ball up in the air, it was clear that no one was going to simply invite me to the game.

My moment to jump in came as the group tackled a kid close to me. Bleeding slightly from his nose the kid jumped up, wiped the blood on his white t-shirt that was browner from dirt and now red from blood, and threw the ball in the air for the next round. By this time I was in the mix chasing kids down and getting in on tackles. After about 15 minutes of play the opportunity came. The ball landed and rolled right next to my feet.

The swarm of kids stood looking at the ball then looking back at me. The time between toss, land, and roll seemed to move in slow motion. During that freeze frame I peeked through the crowd to survey just how far I needed to score a touchdown and how many would be tacklers were standing in my way. Out the corner of my eye toward the end zone, I noticed three young girls standing there watching and giggling.

Without any additional hesitation and catching a few kids off guard, I snatched the ball from the ground and begun my journey through the gauntlet. With the ball in my dominant right hand and heart pounding through my chest, I ran for my life. It seemed like more kids appeared to chase me. Two tacklers actually had me at one point, but their efforts only resulted in the back of my t-shirt being ripped as I streaked down the middle of the field.

I approached the touchdown that was clearly marked by a tree on one end, and a big brown dumpster on the other end. I also noticed the girls again by the touchdown line and as I was running, I veered off from the straight line that I had previously traveled and headed in their direction. Looking behind me I noticed that no one was within ten yards of me, so being caught and tackled was no longer a possibility. I coasted in beyond the tree and scored.

Raising my left hand up in the air, I turned around facing the other kids and began my rendition of the Ickey Shuffle. Named after a well-known football player at that time Ickey Woods of the Cincinnati Bengals, I shuffled my feet to the right while holding the football out to the right, shuffled my feet to the left and held the football out to the left, and finally finished by doing three hops to the right and spiking the football into the ground. To this day this touchdown celebration is considered by many to be the most famous in NFL history. The excitement from my touchdown was short-lived as I was reminded that I now had to run the ball back out and attempt to score at the opposite end of the field.

This by far was no easy task, as kids would spread out in all areas of the field to make sure you had no chance in hell of scoring again. Before running out on my second attempt, one of the girls asked me for my name and with the ball in my hand, I walked over and told her. By this time kids were yelling for me to come on, and as I walked back to face what would soon be my death sentence, I winked at the girl. Ego and pride caused a groundswell inside me and all of a sudden I was invincible. Nothing could stop me from reaching that dumpster. My heart was no longer beating through my chest; I could feel it in my mouth and my toes at the same time.

When the beating in my mouth reached its fastest pace I was off. I dashed out running directly down the middle of the field again and within 15 yards I had two people dragging me down. As I fought for more yardage and trying to free myself, I heard somebody yelling, "Hold him up, hold him up" followed by what felt like a truck hitting me from my right as one of the biggest kids on the field came crashing in on my side, knocking the wind out of me.

Still holding onto the ball, another kid came from behind and hit me. As I fell to the ground, several of the kids piled up on me, and a few began to kick and punch me in my face. The thumps and thuds of sneakers and fists seemed to come out of nowhere. There was a pile of tangled bodies and yet enough space for my face to be targeted and struck with precision. As one punch landed I remember hearing, "Stay the fuck away from my sister, bitch."

I began to cry and as the weight from the pile lightened, I was left on the ground bleeding, bruised, and clutching my stomach. Apparently my mystery puncher wanted more of my blood on his hands, so he called me out. I made the safe but grave decision of refusing to fight back. Instead I ran toward my mother's apartment. As I entered into the apartment, my crying grew louder in order for my mom to hear me. Without seeing me, coming to check on me, or raising a hand to comfort me, she cautioned, "Don't come in here crying Rayshawn for nothing!"

I made my way to the living room where she sat. All I had to do was walk into the room for her to notice the lump on my head, ripped t-shirt, pants with fresh holes in both knees, and the mixture of dirt, blood, and tears on my face. Her response was, "What happened to your clothes? I just bought those?" With no concern for the trauma I was experiencing, she ordered me upstairs to take the clothes off and get ready for a bath. What I would learn in the days following my touchdown and victory dance had nothing to do with speed, Ickey Woods, or girls cheering on the sidelines. The fact that I didn't fight back and stand my ground when I was called out and swung on diminished any glory that would have come from playing the game.

I had unknowingly made myself a target and I would have been better off if I had gotten tackled before scoring. In the many days and months that followed, I was chased home on numerous occasions, punched in the chest, slapped, and ridiculed by a few of the kids that were out there the day of my touchdown. Refusing to fight back resulted in a lack of respect and in me being a target for anyone trying to appear strong. Living in fear in that neighborhood was a hell within hell. Although I had other friends that lived across the yard from me whom to this day I'm still close with, days were filled with anxiety over when and which bully would approach, and even more anxiety over how I would respond.

My friends the Henderson's who lived across the short field who had been long time residents of the projects, advised me to fight back or be subjected to being punked and beat up on daily. After being chased inside my own home, being beat up in my mom's living room, being chased from the bus stop, and at times just being afraid of leaving my porch, I was more tired of the fear than afraid. I recognized that the fear and anxiety had to go, I had enough. One day while at the recreation across the street, I was playing a game of basketball.

Things were going well, and myself along with the other boys were having fun until a group of older boys came walking into the gym. One of the older boys demanded that we give them the ball so they could play. I had the ball in my hand and I refused to give the ball up. A kid by the name of Kenny, who I had previous experience with, became impatient with me and knocked the ball out of my hand. Anger and frustration replaced fear and anxiety, and they prevailed. All of the previous incidents flashed through my mind and I wouldn't be a victim again.

I reached back, pulled forward a clenched fist, and connected with his face. The initial impact shocked me into a state of altered consciousness, and for one split second I felt as if I should run. After all, he had other kids with him and I hadn't forgotten being on the bottom of a pile of them punching and kicking me for doing a lot less. But I stood there fearless and, like me, all of the other kids stood there in disbelief. After Kenny regained his momentum, he came charging in my direction and once within reach, I landed a flurry of punches. Each blow came from a place of anger as a result of being mistreated and each time I connected it was like I was gaining some power I never knew I had.

The reality was that I hadn't been trained to defend myself, so my inexperience soon caught up with me when his momentum and my anger caused me to lose control. Before I could help myself to more of his face, I was on the gymnasium floor with Kenny on top of me. The pounding I was taking seemed to last forever and certainly much longer that the punishment that I dished out. The rec center staff soon broke up the fight, and needless to say I was thankful. I managed to walk away with more than a busted lip and bloodied nose, I walked away with my respect.

From that day forward I never had a problem with Kenny or anyone else in my neighborhood. I had stood up for myself and didn't back down. Although my face hurt, I actually felt great long before the swelling went down and the blood stopped. I had gained what was a necessity in my neighborhood no matter who you were. When we crossed paths again he walked past me and spoke. I didn't have to run home or hide from anybody for any reason. In my neighborhood fisticuffs for a boy my age was commonplace and winning was always the goal, but losing was a reality that I was never afraid to face.

I made one thing clear to any of my adversaries: I will fight and you will regret choosing me as your opponent. Mom even treated me differently once she knew that I was fighting back. One particular fight my mother stood in the window and witnessed my beating. She refused to break it up or come to my rescue. Instead when I came inside, she provided me with ice and shared these words, "Always stick up for yourself son. You're going to be in many battles in your life, and it's important that you stand up for what's right at all times." Those words are still the reason why I continue to stand. As a man, my battles don't involve being chased from the bus stop, or hooks and jabs, but all those things encouraged me to pick my battles and study my opponent as well as my plan of attack.

Back then, no matter who you were, living in the projects was not about living, it was about survival. People did what they could each day to survive and it was never glamorous, easy, or carefree. The longer we lived there, the more the neighborhood became home and our neighbors became family. As a result, we looked out for one another and although we would fight each other, we would also protect each other. Outsiders who didn't live out there would pay dearly for any disrespect towards the folks that lived out there. There's something about having had those experiences and shared in all of that suffering that we recognized in each other.

That recognition caused life long bonds and mutual respect. When we cross paths or have occasions to catch up, we sit back and laugh at the many neighborhood games and reminisce on times gone by. One of our favorite pastimes involved us gathering a group of kids who would run up to closed doors then bang on those doors as hard as we could and take off running before anyone could answer. The game was known as "nigger knocking." Most people in the projects knew the game and so they wouldn't even attempt to answer the door until you banged on it multiple times.

The game was heightened if you were fortunate enough to have a pissed off resident chase you. The game did however come with a stiff penalty if you were caught. The unwritten rule was a butt whipping for anyone caught nigger knocking. There were countless variables that made the game more challenging: dogs, number of people playing, number of people home, synchronization of more than one knocker, and the distance from the door to your escape route. Nothing tested your speed and guts like a pissed off man after a hard day's work or a dog chasing you.

I witnessed many of my friends get caught, tripped up, beaten up, and beat with a belt. Not everybody took a liking to the game and being startled by someone banging on their door. At some point we learned that drug dealers and users in our neighborhood really hated the game. Their hatred stemmed from countless times where we would bang and yell like the police.

If you were using or pushing once that door got banged on, it meant you needed to start flushing your products in order to destroy any evidence of criminal activity. That game cost a lot of people a lot of money and put our safety at risk. The game gained local news attention after an innocent child was struck by a bullet from an angry homeowner's gun, who fired warning shots to scare kids off his doorstep. The incident didn't happen in the projects, and so we continued to play the game. Ingenuity and innovation set in and by that time, certain neighborhoods had put a nasty spin on the game and would get animal feces, wrap it up in newspaper, and set it on fire right before banging on the victim's door.

Upon answering the door, the person would usually try and stomp on the paper to put out the fire only to have just stomped on a shit bomb. Although it was not common for victims to ever call the police, there were times when people did, and children were charged with either trespassing or disturbing the peace. Parents then would have to spend countless hours in courtrooms downtown only for the charges to either be dismissed, or curfew being placed on them. It would be years later as an adult that I would learn the history of the game.

According to research, the game originated in this country 300 years ago during slavery and carried over well into the 19th century. Individuals who served as overseers on southern plantations where they beat errant slaves caught roaming about in places where they shouldn't be, Nigga' knocking began in the post-bellum south. It's been said that white night riders, who soon would be known as the Ku Klux Klan, would go around the colored part of town at night and go door-to-door knocking and whoever answered would be attacked and sometimes lynched.

Out of all the games played in the projects, the most memorable one will always be "Hide & Go Get It." This game was a cross between hide-n-seek and tag, only with a spin. Boy and girls would team up based on gender, and girls would be required to go and hide in various places while the boys attempted to find them.

Boys who found girls were entitled to feel up, rub down, kiss, or even better, grind on the girl. For many of us, this game allowed us a chance to explore sexuality and often times have your first experience with a girl. Once the girls went to hide, the boys would usually have quick discussions on who they were going to find. It was typically girls that they already had crushes on. Most times there was at least one unattractive girl in the crew that nobody wanted to find, and she would often hide in some of the most obvious places wanting to be found.

There was also typically a girl who wanted to be found by anybody and everybody. High-fives were given and stories exchanged with other boys to compare notes. Then we would switch and make sure we found different girls in order to keep it interesting. My most fond memory of this game came one day after a girl I was seeking out hid on the stairwell at the elementary school that was located right inside of the projects. For what felt like an hour, we stood in that stairwell bumping and grinding so hard we could have started a fire.

I looked forward to the next round because I knew she would return to the same hiding spot. It was a hot summer day and I had on shorts with a tank top. I remember finding her on the stairway and standing behind her grinding against her in a circular motion. Now mind you, according to the game's unwritten rules, grinding is only supposed to last for a short period of time. But this time was different for me. As I continued to grind on her, the feeling was so good that I didn't want to stop. My intensity increased and so did my circular motion. Faster and faster I went, holding onto her hips tight to not let her go and after about three minutes, the feeling I experienced was one that will never be forgotten.

It was like I had walked into a room and everybody yelled surprise and gave me the best gift ever. After it was over, instead of running back where the boys were, I took my time walking back trying to figure out what just happened. When I finally reached them they all asked what took me so long getting back. I had no words to explain to them. One of my friends noticed that I had a huge wet spot on the front of my shorts. He said I had pissed myself.

All the boys laughed and didn't want to touch me and while I was confused about what happened, I knew that I hadn't pissed my pants. I went home to examine myself and upon entering the restroom, I had no idea what I was about to witness. As I pulled my pants down to take a look, I noticed a strange fluid was all over me. Indeed it was not piss but since I had never seen it before, I became nervous and concerned. I touched it and didn't like the texture. I brought my hands close to my nose and didn't like the smell of it either, so it must have been something bad.

I immediately took off all of my clothes to bathe. I remember asking myself, "What in the hell just happened to me? Did she give me some kind of disease?" As I was washing up I picked up my shorts and underwear to examine them only to notice that by this time, it was all dried up and crusty. No way could I let my mom see what had just happened, so putting the clothes in the dirty clothes bin was not an option. I ran to my room to put on fresh clothes. Then I crept to the kitchen to find a small trash bag where I wrapped the clothes up and ditched them in the trash never to be seen again.

It would be months before I would engage in that game again. The next time I was approached to play the game, I came up with every excuse as to why I couldn't play. The one that seemed to work the best was that my mom said if she caught me playing she was going to whoop my ass. The kids in the neighborhood knew my mom had a tendency to deliver on that promise and in front of them no less, so that excuse seemed realistic. For a child, as much as the projects were about fun and games, it was also about survival.

I watched firsthand how the concept of survival of the fittest played out. People were very poor and often did whatever it took to survive. Kids as young as 11-years-old were introduced to the dope game. Something as simple as being a runner (taking drugs or money to a specific apartment) or a look-out (keeping an eye out for the police for the neighborhood drug dealer) could produce income, but also be life-altering. During this same time period, pregnant or mothering women could participate in the Women, Infants

& Children (WIC) program. The government subsidy program known as WIC would provide healthy food products to children from birth to the age of five.

Participants would receive a delivery of a crate dropped off on their front porch. The crates consisted of a gallon of milk, a slab of cheese, eggs, cereal, and orange juice. The truck came in the projects at the same time every week and if you were not at home when he knocked on the door, you would come home to find that somebody in the neighborhood had stolen your goods. People got smart and would have somebody be there to catch the delivery so it would not get stolen. I remember seizing the opportunity due to hunger and stealing people's food, taking it home, and my mom never questioning me about it.

I survived living in the projects because I adapted to the culture and took each lesson in stride. I learned to become a sponge and a chameleon taking in my environment and adapting to whatever came my way in order to survive. At the time I was not involved in many delinquent activities, but I learned so much by watching others, including my own mother. Those learned behaviors I would later put to use.

One in thirty-three American children and one in eight African- American children go to sleep each night denied access to a parent because that parent is behind bars. One out of every ten children has a parent that is involved in the criminal justice system, whether in prison, on probation, or on parole. As these numbers continue to rise, the voice of the children who are largely impacted will remain silent. From arrest, to sentencing, to visiting, the impact that the process has on children is devastating and life-changing.

KID OF INCARCERATED PARENT

I had to have been around 6-years-old when I experienced my mother's first run-in with the law. Even at that age I was smart and aware enough to know or suspect that my mom was involved in things that she had no business doing. Times when I was supposed to be upstairs in my bed sleeping, I would often creep to the top of the stairs to listen to her phone calls, or the conversations she was having with people in the living room.

Those conversations would turn out to be the times when she was plotting her next move and discussed the amount of money or property to be gained if she was successful. I also knew that she worked for the neighborhood dope man from time to time selling drugs, but most often allowing them to use our apartment to cook up and then distribute the drugs. Growing up in an apartment like this meant that the daily traffic would often bring folks in and out of my environment that I would normally be told to stay away from. It was always the same story of my mother passing him off as a friend from high school.

These men would endear themselves to me by calling me little man and occasionally slap boxing with me, and it always ended the same when I would be promised a bike, clothes, or toys the next time they saw me. Not knowing any better, my excitement about the possibility of getting those things would grow along with anticipation. No matter what was promised or what was said it was like clockwork--I'd see them again and they would pass right by me like they didn't even know me.

No gift, and most times, not even the "Hey lil' man" that I had grown accustomed to. What they did consistently provide was the constant fear that existed in my mother's apartment, which was supposed to be my home.

The smell of cooked crack cocaine became as regular as hearing "Honey, I'm home" on the TV shows I watched. My nights were filled with sleeplessness and sleep interrupted by yelling, cursing, banging at the door, and conversations about who owed who money. I typically wouldn't fall asleep until I knew the house was completely empty and mom was upstairs in her bed.

On one particular night, I was awakened by several loud knocks at the front door followed by a boom so loud I thought it was a gunshot. As I jumped up from my bed in fear, I heard men screaming, "Everybody get down! Columbus Police!" Several police officers could be heard storming inside followed by the yells of my mother telling them she had a son upstairs. As I stood at the top of the stairs screaming and yelling, an officer appeared, and instead of comforting me he yelled, "Let me see your hands!"

I remember throwing my hands in the air as he walked up the stairs. I also remember not seeing his face because all I could see was the barrel of his gun pointed at me. He also asked me if anyone else was upstairs, buy fear didn't allow me to speak. I tried to say no, but words wouldn't leave my mouth, so instead I shook my head in indication. Two more officers followed to search the apartment and ensure that I was telling the truth. Once they realized I was alone, one of the officers picked me up and carried me downstairs.

As he walked me through the kitchen towards the door, he stepped over my mom and two other men who were cuffed and laid face down on the floor. I recognized the other two because over the past two months, they had been there what seemed like every night. The SWAT officers were dressed in all black with masks covering their faces, and the sight of a gun pointed at my mom while she was lying face down placed me in a state of panic. I started to cry uncontrollably as I was led to one of the police cruisers and placed in the backseat. What seemed like hours passed and nobody came to check on me to see if I was okay.

I remained in the backseat of that cruiser crying with my face pressed against the window, waiting to see if anything would give an indication of what was taking place inside of the apartment. Although it was extremely late and dark, the lights from sirens and headlights lit up our complex like Christmas. As more time passed, I could see police officers standing around talking and laughing. I wondered what could be funny at a time when I was so terrified that I almost peed my pants. Through the windows of our home, I could see officers upstairs and downstairs tearing through my mother's things.

It seemed as if their goal was to tear up everything in the apartment the way they were turning over furniture and knocking things over that couldn't possibly conceal anything. It was as though they were done looking for drugs, so they just decided to trash our home. I remained in the back of the police car through this whole process. My tears had stopped, but I was still frightened. I began to wonder where I would be taken. Was I going to jail? Was I under arrest too? I could see the neighbors peeking out their windows watching like it were some sort of action packed suspense movie. It seemed like hours before I finally witnessed my mom being escorted out in handcuffs by two masked officers.

I could see tears running down her face, which hurt me even more and caused my fear to intensify and the tears once again began to flow. For a brief second our eyes met as she passed my line of sight. I pounded on the glass, yelled for her, and followed her path with my eyes until she was out of sight again. Soon after, the other two men were escorted out of the apartment and placed in separate police cars. Still no one came to check on me or showed any concern for how scared I was.

When one finally did come, he sat in the front seat and made a few calls back and forth over his radio. While waiting on a response from the lady on the other end, he looked at me through his rearview mirror and asked, "Hey buddy, do you know those two guys your mom was at the house with?"

Trying to catch my breath from crying so much, I responded by telling the officer that I didn't know their names but they had been there before. Before he could get the next question out, I asked him where they were taking me and if my mom was coming back home tonight. As if what I had experienced wasn't bad enough, his response devastated my six-year-old mind even more. He let out a big sigh, shook his head and said, "I'm not sure your mom is coming home anytime soon." Those words sent me over the edge, and I remember yelling for them to bring my mom back while I kicked the back of the seat and pounded the window that separated the officer from me.

He ignored my screams, pleas, and tears and carried on with his duties. Meanwhile the other officers where turning off the lights in the apartment and began to close and lock the doors. I watched the police cruisers slowly drive away with my mom in the backseat. Two officers then approached the car and walked me back inside to pick out clothes that I would take with me. As I walked in, I remember looking at our home thinking my mom would never let it be this way. It was worse than I originally thought: the furniture was turned over, things were pulled out of the cabinets, and pictures were removed from the walls.

As I reached the top step I glanced into my mom's room and noticed the bed had been turned over and all of her clothes thrown on the floor. My room was no different. I stood there and wondered why the police officers would do this to my room; I was just a little kid. I stepped over clothes and toys to begin finding what I would take when my heart sank as I took notice to my broken *Speak and Spell*. A boot print was left where the screen once was.

Along with the sense of security that my room provided, my youth was also taken from me that night and I would grow very accustomed to the way I would feel that night. After being rushed, grabbing a change of clothes and getting changed out of my pajamas, I was then escorted back into the police car that would eventually transport me to Franklin County Children Services. Once in the building, I was then led to a very bright, small, and cold room with a small cot and simply told to wait there.

I was provided a thin blanket and a pillow, which smelled like some other scared kid hadn't been able to control his bladder like I did. The smell of piss and the hum of the bright light were the backdrop as I cried myself to sleep. I lay there feeling like I had done something wrong and whether I had or hadn't, the outcome was not about to change. I was alone, afraid, and didn't know what tomorrow would bring. The next morning, I woke up to unfamiliar white faces that sat around discussing my placement. It seemed like hours before I knew that I would be moved into a temporary foster home with a couple until they determined where I would be going from there.

Once I arrived, I didn't say as much as a word and I was soon led to a room. I sat down on the twin bed and observed my surroundings. The room was clean, neat, and very calming. The television caught my eye because I wasn't accustomed to having one in any room that I slept in. Across the room was another twin bed and it was clear that I would not be in this room alone. My attention was diverted when I was called down by the caseworker.

She formerly introduced me to the white couple that politely extended a warm, welcoming greeting to me. I was told my stay would be short, but depended on how soon a more permanent placement could be identified, or if a family member indicated that they would be willing to care for me. Mr. and Mrs. Smith began to ask questions about my likes and dislikes and showed me around the rest of their home. Although I appreciated the clean house and living space, I was still apprehensive about the Smiths. I even felt a bad vibe from them despite no wrongdoing on their part.

The way Mr. Smith looked at me when no one was around made me feel uncomfortable. I had grown used to the back and forth small talk, play fighting, and actually looked forward to male interaction, but this guy was different. Maybe my mind didn't allow me to go there once I found out he was a police officer? Either way, I had no intentions of getting comfortable with him or in their home, or a few days into my stay my suspicions were validated. Most children have a sixth sense when it comes to adults, and I was no different.

I was taking a bath one night when Mr. Smith came into the bathroom to check on me. He asked if I were okay staying with them and if I needed anything. While he was talking to me, I noticed that his eyes did not leave from the tub area. Since I had already been in the tub for a while, the bubbles that once covered my lower half had begun to disappear, leaving me exposed. It didn't take me long to realize that Mr. Smith was staring inside the tub, past the water and bubbles to my penis.

He sat on the toilet continuing to make small talk as I attempted to close my legs in hopes of blocking his view. He asked me if I was done washing up and once I said that I was, he reached over and grabbed my towel. As I slowly stood up from the water, I tried to crouch down as low as I could so that my private parts weren't exposed to his fixed gaze. Once I was upright, I was sure that he would get up and make his way to the door to give me some privacy. For as much as I hoped that would happen, it didn't. As I stepped both feet out of the tub, he just sat there with the towel in hand.

He unfolded it and when I went to reach for the towel, he wrapped it around me and started to dry me off. He started at my calves and worked his way up to my penis. He stayed there attempting to dry an already dry area for what felt like an eternity. A different type of fear came over me, it wouldn't let me move. My inability to move and uncertainty about his intentions meant that I was just standing there immobile. Relief came when I heard his wife calling his name and approaching from the stairs. It was even clearer to me that he knew he was doing something wrong when he jumped up, dropped the towel and tip-toed out of the bathroom before his wife could see what was going on.

I stood there not knowing what to do or say. However, I did know that it did not feel good, I didn't like it, and it wasn't right. I could hear small talk between them both. I stood there drying the rest of my body as quickly as I could and as I turned to reach for my underwear, I felt his eyes on me again. The door made a creaking noise and there he stood staring at me through the small opening. Once he saw that I noticed him he slowly pulled the door shut. I stayed in the bathroom fully dressed until I thought it was safe to leave.

I felt like I was about to face a monster in the hallway and if I could just make it into the bed and under the covers, I would be safe. So with every bit of speed and courage I could gather, I dashed across the hallway to the bedroom, closed the door behind me, and jumped into bed. I held the covers so tight that night that my hands hurt the next day. Unfortunately, sleep did not come and I would spend the next few nights in a state of restlessness out of concern for Mr. Smith coming into any room I was in or watching me with those dirty looks.

I even learned to bathe before he came home from work. On nights that I was unable to bathe prior to him coming home, I would find a way to already have my pajamas on to appear as if I had already bathed. Going to bed dirty was a small price to pay for the sense of security that I was able to hold on to, even if it was just for another day. I was sure he could sense the discomfort I felt resulting from his sick attempts at bath time, and most times he couldn't even look me in my face.

I would stay with the Smith's for almost thirty days, and soon the same woman who placed me there was standing in the living room to pick me back up. My mom had been released and I was returning home. As I came downstairs with my few belongings, including some clothes they had brought me, the lady smiled and asked me if I was ready to go. With a smile on my face as big as the hug I planned to give my mother, I approached her and planned to continue my pace towards the door.

She then stopped my momentum and asked how my stay with the Smith's had been. Mrs. Smith began to tell her how much of a pleasure it was to have me, and how much of a great kid I was. The entire time I was making eye contact with Mr. Smith. Everything in me wanted to tell both ladies what a pervert he was and how he made me feel, but the look on his face said, "You better not say a word" and quite honestly, I was scared. Instead, I told the worker that I was fine but couldn't wait to get home to my mother.

That fateful night when the police came knocking taught the six- year-old me three things: my mom was bad and a criminal, police officers were monsters who used their power to instill fear, and I was a bad kid. It would be years before I experienced another humiliating experience resulting from my mother's lifestyle. I was a junior in high school staying in my last foster home before children services emancipated me to my own apartment. I was lying in my bed right before the eleven o'clock news. I switched back and forth from one station to the other, with both anchormen providing background on the "Breaking News" story as I listened.

A woman had been arrested for conning elderly people out of thousands of dollars, and robbing them once she was able to gain access into their homes. The woman was posing as a part of President Bill Clinton's Healthcare Program staff. Once she was inside their homes, she would find a way to take anything of value that she could. It wasn't too long before they showed the picture of the accused, and I saw my mom's mug shot and name front and center on my TV screen. I immediately sat up in my bed in shock and disbelief as they continued with the story.

A couple of interviews from victims were shown as they talked about the items that came up missing in their homes. It had been a few months since I talked to my mom and I had no idea what she was doing. The story seemed like it ran forever. As I attempted to turn to another station to escape that reality, it followed me. The story was on every channel I turned to and without hesitation, I snatched the cord from the wall. I had a hard time sleeping that night and I remember having thoughts of my childhood experience when the police took her away from me for that thirty-day period.

Lack of sleep and vision blurred from tears seemed to be recurring theme in my life but despite that, I managed to make it to the bus stop on time. My first period class was English and every morning in that class the teacher would read stories from the local newspaper, and we would have class discussions about the current event. The teacher went over a few national stories before turning his attention to local news. He began reading the front page of the metro section. I sat there in my seat filled with emotion as he read the story of my mother's crimes aloud for everyone to hear.

No one knew it was my mother, but I knew it, and it hurt. Not even at school could I escape. I couldn't unplug my teacher, or silence his words. I attempted to drown him out with the noise in my mind, but somehow I was able to hear his words as he got to the end of the article. He read, "If convicted, she could face up to 15 years in state prison." Hearing those words and the possibility of being away from my mom drove me over the top at that very moment.

I jumped up from my desk, screamed in anger, and picked up the empty desk that was in front of me and threw it across the room. I stormed out of the room and punched every locker in my path. My vision was blurred again as I made my way out of the front of the building. Once outside, I collapsed onto the sidewalk and lay there and cried. The scene I created caused school administrators and teachers to come running to check on me.

Sadness was replaced by anger, and I wasn't in a position to talk to anyone about my outburst. I could hear the English teacher in the background telling the principal what happened, and then I heard my favorite math teacher Ms. Robertson say, "Oh my God, that's his mother." I had developed a relationship with Ms. Robertson, who had taken a special interest in me and spent extra time tutoring me in math. In between individual help sessions, I would open up to her and tell her about my life. For the first time ever, I felt like I found someone who understood me, and hearing her voice calmed my anger.

Her hugs and reassuring hand on my back led me back into the building. I was able to regain my composure for that day, but in the weeks to come I was an emotional wreck. I learned my mom was indeed sentenced to prison for not only the charges that were brought up on the news, but also for charges that her own sister pressed against her. Prior to her being sent away to prison, I went to see my mother at the county jail. Seeing her from behind a glass wall and hearing her voice through a muffled phone was hard for me.

Despite what she was in trouble for, I still wanted to hold and hug her. She was my mother and I loved her. I somehow felt like if I could just hug her at that moment, things would be okay. She never cried or showed any emotion while I was there, and I will never know what emotional state she was in. Was she embarrassed? Upset? Saddened or regretful? I still can't say, but I know it was pretty rough on me and those are still some of the most vivid memories of my adolescence. Those visits proved to be too much for me. Going to see her was hard all by itself, but leaving her there when our time was up was so hard, it made the thought of visiting with her sickening.

I would leave the county jail with my face streaked with tears, and those tears turned into sleepless nights, which carried over into my school days. I started to miss a lot of school and when I wasn't missing school, my sadness wouldn't allow me to focus on anything academic. I daydreamed in class for hours at a time, and when visions of her face behind bars would appear, I'd put my head down at my desk to shed a few private tears. For years I felt a sense of abandonment, and knowing that she was headed to prison for a long time only heightened those feelings.

Being in foster care was one thing because I knew there was a possibility of us reuniting, but knowing she was headed to prison was another because there was no possibility of me going back home, or being able to be with my mother for whatever time a judge and prosecutor decided. The letters she would write always left me depressed. Some letters would come and as a defense mechanism, I wouldn't open them. I would just put them under my mattress.

My anger, sadness, and resentment wouldn't allow me to go visit her while she was incarcerated and despite her pleas, I never made my way to Marysville Correctional Institution. It wasn't that I didn't want to see her, I just knew it would always be extremely difficult to leave her behind. Years would go by without any face-to- face contact. Once my mother served her time and was finally transferred to the Pre-Release Correctional Facility located just fifteen minutes or less from me, we planned a visit.

Mother's Day 2006, the facility planned a very nice event where kids and family could come and take part in a variety of activities. The menu was full of food items that typically were not served: fried chicken, mac and cheese, greens and corn bread made the day feel extra special. It felt good to see her that day, to hold her, hug her, and most importantly, to hear three words come from her mouth that I had not heard in what seemed like years.

As she hugged me tight before I left the facility she whispered, "I love you" in my ear. I had no idea those would be the last words I would ever hear her say to me. She passed away later that year due to a number of health complications.

"Blood makes you related, but Loyalty makes you family."
~Rayshawn

FOSTER HOMES/GROUP HOMES

My introduction into Franklin County Children Services came at a very young age, when my mom became very ill with her asthma and was hospitalized for over six months. At the time, no one in my family would take me in, claiming that they didn't have room because their own children were still living at home. As a result, Children Services was called and I was placed with a single mom named Pam and her son, Shay.

When I first arrived at the nice townhome, I was very nervous to be in a place other than my own. Many nights it was hard for me to sleep because it was always too quiet in the neighborhood. There was no loud music, nobody outside my bedroom window yelling or fighting, no gunshots or sirens, just too quiet to the point that I thought something was wrong. In the days to come, I grew to feel safe being there. Pam and Shay really made me feel at home.

I experienced my first Christmas while I was there and I will always remember those days leading up to it. It was quite different for me considering that my mom and I had practiced the Muslim religion in which we didn't celebrate Christmas. I remember the day being awakened by Shay, who was a few years younger than me. He pulled the covers from over my head pushing me to wake up, "Get up Rayshawn! It's Christmas and Santa has been here!!"

I rolled over towards the window and noticed that it was still dark outside and attempted to pull the covers back over me, not at all impressed by some man that I thought only came to a select few of homes. As eager and persistent as Shay was he refused to allow me to go back to sleep. Half sleep I rolled out of the bed while he pulled me by the arms down the stairs. As I walked down the stairs, I was able to see the most amazing thing. The Christmas tree was bright, filled with colorful blinking lights. What almost made my heart stop was what I noticed under the tree. There had to have been over twenty presents under the tree.

In shock, I remember just standing in the living room in awe and amazement, not even knowing which presents were mine. The noise awakened Pam and she soon came down the stairs. I was too nervous to touch anything, considering that my mom had beat it into my brain that Santa Claus didn't exist and would never be coming for me. She grabbed my hand, walked me closer to the tree, and picked up a gift that had my name on it. I don't remember all of the presents that I was given, but I do recall just being so overwhelmed.

That was just one of the few days that will always stick out to me about living with them. It always touched me how she gave me so much love by hugging me, and telling me how smart and handsome I was. Those were simple words that I just was not used to hearing from my mom. She provided me with an environment that was welcoming and most importantly it was safe. She offered stability and I never had to worry about food, so in the end, I grew to trust her. Although I was a few years older than Shay, I grew to enjoy the brotherly relationship that was developing. Just like any younger sibling, he wanted to go where I went and never wanted to be apart from me.

Over the next several months my relationship with the family strengthened and I felt comfortable. I had no worries living with them, but always wondered how long I would stay with them. After almost a year, my time with them had come to an end. Mom was feeling better and had satisfied all of the requirements on the case plan in order to get me home. Although I was happy that she was healthier, I was not at all thrilled about returning home with her. I would be going back to uncertainty, to instability, to fear, and to the constant yelling and screaming that she often did.

I voiced my concern about not wanting to go back. Pam attempted to try and keep me. In the end, the courts returned me back to my mom. Pam and Shay kept in touch with me as much as they could for some time. I visited them every now and then, but it just wasn't the same. My mom moved around a few times after I returned home and I lost contact with Pam and Shay. Having no way of getting in contact with them, I lost hope that I would ever see them again. It would be a few years later before I would have my second experience with being placed in a foster home. By this time, my mother's addiction to crack had grown progressively worse, and her inability to care for my younger brother and me became clear to family and friends.

Someone had called Children Services and they began to investigate her abuse and neglect in the home. There was a man that used to come by our apartment from St. Stephens Community Center to provide some services for us. A slim gentleman that was always kind and polite to me, he knew the challenges that we faced inside the home. I informed him that children services was investigating and that I was sure to be removed from the home at some point. He asked me about other relatives that could take me and I assured him that although I had a few aunts that lived here, they were not willing to take me, just like they hadn't a few years ago.

I could see the look of concern in his eyes, but I had no idea if or how he could help. During the investigation period, I remember me and my mom getting into many heated arguments about various things, which often led to me running away from home for a few days. I would sometimes stay at various friends' houses, or at that time I had a girlfriend whose mom didn't mind me staying the night. It wouldn't be too long after the investigation opened that my brother and me were removed from the home. My brother was lucky and was placed with my great-aunt whom he had spent much time with anyway.

I had no idea where I was going to be placed until I reached the Children Services building to see the tall slim guy from St. Stephens smiling and waiting for me. Shocked yet excited to see him, I smiled as well as my children services worker informed me that Ron was willing to care for me for a while. They asked me a series of questions, making sure I was okay with the move, and I was. I had grown to love seeing Ron come around to our house. I enjoyed the few times we were able to hang out together.

Ron was a single man in his early 30's who loved working with children and passionate about helping families. By the time I started living with Ron, I had already attended two middle schools, one being Heritage Middle School where I was expelled a short time before. During a science class while the teacher was not in the room, I decided to set the trashcan on fire.

Before the teacher could return to the room, I had managed to put the fire out. When the teacher returned he asked the class who was burning something, and no one raised their hand for fear of retaliation. The teacher then informed the class that he would be making himself available for students to come forward after class. In the end, almost all of my white classmates pointed me out as the culprit. School officials decided to file charges on me for inducing panic in school.

I was placed on probation, ordered to attend a fire starters program, and was told I could never attend any Westerville public schools again. The thought of going to another middle school created some excitement, yet anxiety of having to start all over again. However, this was nothing new considering I had gone to three elementary schools. Ron had a nice apartment located in a decent neighborhood on the east side of Columbus. My relationship with Ron grew and I became comfortable living with him. I looked up to him and over the course of several months, I viewed him as the father figure I've always wanted. To tell the truth, I felt that way about him from the onset of our interactions.

After several months of living with Ron things all of a sudden began to take a turn for the worst. On numerous occasions, Ron had asked me to not have friends in the house while he was gone. For the most part I respected that and would have a few friends over and we stayed outside. On one particular day, one of my friends needed to use the restroom and didn't want to walk the few blocks to his home. He begged me to let him come inside to use the restroom because it was starting to sprinkle with rain.

He promised that he wouldn't stay in there long and would be out of the apartment in good enough time before Ron even made it home. I let him in and he used the restroom and we sat on the couch waiting for the rain to let up so that he could get home. While watching TV, we were cracking up in stitches at the screen when his foot lifted up under one of the glass coffee tables and broke the entire glass. We both sat there in shock at what had just happened.

As we were sitting there stunned, I soon heard the keys turning in the door indicating that Ron had come home early. His apartment was designed with only one way in and one way out, so running out a back door was not an option. As he walked up the steps I could do nothing but sit there and look at my friend with the "shit about to get real" look. The look of disappointment expressed on his face when he entered the room is one I would never forget. He didn't yell or scream, but politely asked my friend to leave. He ordered me to pick the glass up carefully and he went to his room and shut the door.

It was a few hours before he came out of his room to talk to me. He asked me again not to have anyone inside the house while he was not there. I was very apologetic and explained to him what happened. Months followed with me having other behavioral problems in school and at home. Although I enjoyed going to school, I struggled in many classes, which meant that during class I would find other ways to occupy my time. I was once suspended from school for accidentally hitting the teacher on the side of the face with a spitball that was intended for a classmate who dodged the incoming wet ball that hit the teacher instead. My grades were always mainly D's and F's and Ron spent really no time helping me with work, although encouraging me with words to do better.

I was not involved in anything in the community to occupy my time, although I loved going to the skating rink, especially during the all night skate. It appeared Ron didn't mind taking me to the skating rink until one night I overheard a phone conversation he was having with one his friends. It appeared that he was invited to go out somewhere that he really wanted to go to and I heard him tell somebody that he couldn't go because he had to make sure this bad ass kid made to it the skating party, and he wasn't sure how much longer he was going to be able to do this with me.
I grew up hearing the saying that "sticks and stones may break your bones, but words don't hurt."

That was a complete lie as hearing those words made me angry. The excitement that I had about going skating was all but lost, and the ride there was very quiet. I could tell that he was not at all excited about driving me all the way to the north side from the east side of Columbus, and having to come back to pick me up in just a few short hours. It wasn't too much longer before one day I came home from school with my clothes being packed up and Ron telling me that Children Services had made "other" arrangements for me.

My next stop landed me in the cottages known back then as Franklin Village. A series of different cottages full of young kids, many African-American boys, waiting to be placed either back home, in another group home, or other placement. During this time period, I was not enrolled in school and had not had any contact with my family members. I remember being so uncomfortable there with several other youth that I didn't know.

I was showed to my room with at least two other boys. I remember the room smelling like pee, and just the cottage itself was unkempt. The group home workers provided me with very little direction, and I relied on others who had been there for days to show me the ropes. Fighting was common in the cottage and it was typically over food. I quickly established myself as the one not to play with one day when I got up from my plate to get a paper towel. As I turned around, I noticed a boy had reached over on my plate and grabbed some food. I walked over to him, asked for it back, and not only did he refuse but he proceeded to place the food in his mouth with a slight smile.

While he was still chewing, I grabbed him by his throat and slammed him to the ground continuing to choke him. He spit the food out and before I could punch him in his face, several people came to break it up. I was then removed from that cottage and transferred. My frustration continued to grow with being there. I asked to speak to my caseworker and I was informed that she was no longer my caseworker, and I would be assigned one soon. I would spend almost a month and a half there before finally being told that I was being placed in a new group home.

I was going to be the first person to enter the group home on the north side of Columbus, an area in which I had never lived. It seemed like the drive to the group home took forever. I was excited to be leaving the Village, although I was nervous and apprehensive about my new location. Somehow I managed to reach the 9th grade, so I was also excited about that and be attending Brookhaven High School. Brookhaven was a very well known and popular high school at the time. I sat in complete silence the whole ride there, deciding not to engage in small talk with a caseworker I had just met. I had no intentions of getting to know her because in my mind, once I was dropped off, I knew the odds of us interacting on a regular basis would be slim.

At this point I had grown to just accept that caseworkers come and go and with me, I usually only spoke with them if there was a problem. Anything she was trying to say to me at that the time meant nothing to me. As we pulled up to the little white house that had a fence around it, the only thing that I was excited about was the fact that I would be the first and only one in the group home until more referrals came in. As we walked in, I was greeted by a middle-aged white woman and one of the group home workers, who was a black male. Everyone was excited to have me there as the first occupant of the home. I sat on one end of the couch with my one bag of clothes next to me as I listened to the caseworker and the staff talk about me as if I weren't there.

They made all these plans and talked about what was best for me, but not once did anyone turn to ask me what it was that I wanted and what I thought was best for me. I was given a list of rules that included chores to be done, and at the end of the week I would be given five dollars for allowance. After the usual bullshit conversation that I typically had with caseworkers, she provided her contact information if I ever needed anything and then rushed off to deal with the next kid. I took in the surroundings of my new home and was quite impressed. It was clean, had new furniture, and appeared to be in a decent neighborhood.

Upon the owners departure, the group home worker finally approached me with, "What's up little nigga? You just gone sit there and not talk?" I told him I didn't have shit to say and to show me where my room was. After I was settled in, we walked across the street where they had another group home for younger kids. That group home was already filled with five boys. It didn't take long before I was sharing space with other boys my own age after one boy that I remembered from the Village arrived about two months after I did.

The once quiet house settled in a quiet neighborhood, was quiet no more. The group home appeared to have no real screening process in terms of whom they accepted. Kids came and went for multiple reasons and so did the group home workers, who were primarily African-American men in their early 30's. Me and another kid were the only two stable kids that had been long standing at the group home, so we typically ran the place and got first dibs on clothes and food.

When other kids left, I would end up keeping their lunch tickets then going to school and selling them for discounted prices to the kids that had to pay for their lunches. Soon, the five dollars a week I was getting for allowance didn't mean much as I was able to rack up almost $50 a week secretly selling lunch tickets. I would soon find out that I was not the only hustler in that group home. I found out that some of the group home workers were somehow hustling money with clothing vouchers that were supposed to be spent on kids, and they were spending it on themselves.

Once I found out, I made it known to them that I knew and demanded that they cut me in on clothes or else I was going to the CEO. It was no problem for them to give me what I wanted. While I was there, I learned a hard lesson with respect to girls. I had been in a relationship with a girl that I had known for a few years, and one of the group home workers would drive me to pick her up and allow her to spend the night with me on numerous occasions. The group home worker knew how much I cared for this girl and he could see that I would go out of my way to see her.

During that time of my life, she was the only person that I held close to me. I could always depend on her when I needed her, even during those times when I needed to run away from home. I remember one day when the group home worker sat me down and told me that I was spending too much time with this girl and she was going to hurt me. I told him that Angel was not like that and she would never do anything to hurt me. With a smirk on his face I remember him responding, "You don't know shit about women, so let me tell me something. These bitches out here can never be trusted, and don't ever think you're the only one. And don't you ever think that your girl can't be got by another man, because she can." I told him that he didn't know what he was talking about and that Connie wasn't like the rest of them.

A few weeks later after getting off the bus, I walked in the front door of the group home and noticed Connie sitting there on the couch. I was confused because I had not called her, nor did we have plans to see each other. Before I could open my mouth to say a word, the group home worker was walking out the staff bedroom putting his pants back on. I asked Connie what she was doing here and she sat there in stunned silence. My eyes filled with tears, my heart filled with anger and hurt as I looked at her then at him. I then ran out of the group home crying my heart out.

With nowhere to go, I ran across the street by the police station and sat on the curb crying with my head in my lap. The one person, the one woman that I trusted hurt me and it was just too hard to accept. I lifted my head in the direction of the group home and could see the group home worker kissing her as he reached for her hand. They walked out the house and got into his car so he could drop her back off at home.

Later that day I stayed in my room still upset when the group home worker tried to come and talk to me. He sat down on my bed and told me that it was not his intent to hurt me, but to teach me a lesson about women so when I got older I would understand how to deal with them. During that conversation I remember him telling me, "Man always has a weakness and if you ever want to truly get to a man, go for what is closest to his heart, which is more than likely going to be a woman and his money. Never trust the two because you will find yourself more loyal to them than they are to you. It's always a lopsided relationship."

In the days and months to come, that group home worker exposed me to a variety of situations with him interacting with women. I watched him and his brother, who was also a group home worker, run trains on women and they would even allow me to be involved. The women never resisted. Here I was, this 15-year-old boy being with women who were sometimes twice my age. It didn't bother me one bit. As a matter of fact, it was fun and exciting to get the attention considering that girls didn't pay me any attention at school.

The environment at the group home drastically changed over the course of my stay there. The house became ran down, fights took place almost daily, and the group home workers were just as shady as the kids that were there. I would stay in that group home close to a year before it was closed down. Those group home workers I would not see again until my adult years. Prior to the group home's closing, Connie came to visit me a few times, but I would only allow her to come when that particular staff member wasn't around. Although I was hurt, I didn't allow that to stop me from having sex with her, and I showed none of the emotion that I usually gave her.

I had sex with her out of anger, and releasing was simply for my enjoyment. I would have sex with her several times before leaving the group home with no intentions of seeing her again. After the group home closed, I was placed in two other foster homes with black men, one being from Nigeria. By the time I was at the last group home, I had attended three elementary schools, four middle schools, and was now entering into my fourth high school at Independence High School. The only thing that I was excited about with going to this high school is that I would be reconnected with some old friends from one of the middle schools I had previously attended. By this time I was going on 17-years-old. Going into my last foster home, I wondered how long it would be before I would end up moving again.

At this school, my focus was strictly on girls and playing football. I was living with a man who had such a kind heart and could hardly speak English. He provided some of the best meals I ever had having never eaten African food. I followed the rules he set forth in the beginning, but I soon realized it was a whole world waiting on me, and abiding by curfew was limiting my options. The relationship with him soon went south when he came home early to find a naked woman about five years my senior and me in his apartment getting down. He told me that I needed to contact my caseworker and find somewhere else to stay.

At 17-years-old, they were not about to try and place me at another foster home and move me away from the high school I was attending. My caseworker sat me down one day and introduced me to a program of emancipation. In this program, they would place me in my own apartment, pay all of my bills for six months, and provide me with a small stipend each month. That was music to my ears and I was eagerly excited to sign up. It didn't take long before I found a studio apartment that was right behind my last foster home. After I was placed in this apartment with my furniture, I hardly ever saw anybody from Children Services.

Nobody really came to check on me with the emancipation worker spending all of 15 minutes with me each month. He asked me a few questions, dropped my check off, and kept moving. And honestly, I was okay with that. It was all fun and exciting to be in high school and, having my own apartment. I often bragged that I had my own place, which was an open invitation to girls. I was headed into my senior year surprisingly on pace to graduate despite my overall GPA being 2.1. I always did just enough to play football.

During my senior year of playing football, I received my first college letter for recruitment from Bluffton University. With at least 18 seniors on the football team, most of us had aspirations of going to college to play football, myself included. However, the lack of guidance and support soon caught up with me. The six months had come to an end with Children Services paying my rent and providing stipend funds. Nobody had taught me how to pay bills or manage my money. By this time I was really struggling in school, particularly in math. On prom night, my principal told me that I had not passed the math portion of the proficiency test that was needed in order to graduate on time. My life was folding before my eyes, and I had nobody to turn to for advice or guidance. Knowing that I had no chance of graduating on time due to failing grades as well, I simply stopped going to school and focused on surviving. The game was calling me and I had no choice but to play.

"Good things may come to those who wait, but only the things left by those who hustle"
~Author Unknown

HINDSITE

Graduating on time with my classmates wasn't a possibility because of my inability to pass the Ohio Proficiency tests and with that realization, I focused my attention on surviving and finding a way to maintain my home. The six-month period covered by the housing program went by quickly and it was soon time to pay that rent each month out of my own pocket. I lived on the East Side of Columbus in an area close to Hamilton Road. The area had every fast food chain you could think of: McDonalds, Burger King, Taco Bell, and even Rally's. That strip had it all.

After I made the decision to stop going to school regularly, I took a few days and spent my time walking up and down Hamilton Road applying for jobs. Time after time I was told that either they were not hiring, or they would keep my application on file for a period of time just in case something came open. In the meantime, the light bill was due. The cable bill soon followed that, but more important, my refrigerator was just about empty and I didn't have much to quiet the stomach grumblings.

From time to time I would walk behind my apartment to the last foster home in which I had lived. I would ask to eat a meal there and he would also give me a few dollars to help me out. But that money would soon disappear. One particular day as I was walking out of his apartment heading back to my own, I felt the vibrations of loud music coming from a car. The trunk rattled like there was something strong on the inside fighting to get out. The music was clear and the words of Tupac's "Me Against The World" could be heard across the parking lot. At the time, Tupac was one of my favorite rappers, and still is today. Many of the songs on that album touched me in many ways because I felt like they spoke to my story and my current situation.

As I nodded my head to the beat of the music and walked in that direction, I realized there was more that demanded my attention. I fixed my eyes on the car that provided the soundtrack to my story and noticed a thing of beauty. There in front of my eyes sat a shiny 1991 Cadillac Deville, powder blue in color with chrome Dayton rims with brown leather interior, or peanut butter guts as we referred to them. As I got closer I expected some grown man to get out of the car, instead it was a young cat that appeared to be around my age.

He stepped out with the latest Jordan's on, gold herringbone chain around his neck, and a pager on his waistband. He let the music bump as he walked past me and I could feel the vibration from the speakers as I got closer. The bass hit so hard, the stereo began to set off a few car alarms. We made eye contact and he spoke, "Sup nigga?" in a friendly tone followed by the universal head nod. After we exchanged greetings, he asked if I knew Tasha who lived in these apartments. I sure did know her.

Tasha was one of the baddest chicks around, but she hardly spoke to anyone, so figuring out whom she was dating was almost impossible. In the Fountain Park East apartments, all of the kids were close and protective of each other, especially with the few girls that lived close by. He introduced himself as Shannon and said he was from California, but been in Ohio for a few years. After a few minutes of small talk I asked if I could sit in his car and listen to a song on the Tupac album. He agreed and I pointed him in the direction of Tasha's apartment. I picked up the cover of the album and opened it up and started to browse through the songs.

After skipping through a few tracks after listening to some verses, I came across track number seven titled "Heavy In The Game", featuring Richy Rich. From the moment the song came on, the bass from the speakers was hypnotizing and I could feel the vibration from my toes to my teeth. I leaned forward in my seat bobbing my head to the beat and listening to the words of the song as if Tupac were talking to me. I instantly blocked everything out and focused directly on the lyrics of the first verse:

*Now how can I explain how this game laced me, plus with
this fame I got enemies do anything to break me, my attitude
changed Got to the point where I was driven, twenty-
four/seven Money's my mission, just a nigga trying to make
a living These busta tricks don't want no mail
They spending they riches on scandalous bitches who'll stay
petrified in jail It's hell, plus all the dealers want a meal ticket
Jealous-ass bitches, player-hating but we still kick it Always
keep my eyes on the prize, watch the police Seen so much
murder, neighborhoods getting no sleep But still, I get my
money on major, continuously Communicating through my
pager, niggaz know me Don't have no homies cause they
jealous, I hustle solo Cause when I'm broke I got no time for
the fellas, listen Ain't nothing poppin 'bout no broke nigga,
ain't no joke Fuck what they say and get your dough nigga
Heavy in the game*

So many parts of that verse set into my thoughts and
helped me believe that life was about hustling 24/7, making
money was the overall mission in life and nothing else
mattered. Getting in the game and staying heavy in the
game while keeping an eye out for the police was the motto.
It spoke to me, telling me "Ain't nothing funny about being
broke, so fuck what ANYBODY is saying, get out there in
those streets make that money, and just stay heavy in the
game."

That verse did something to me. It was so impactful I
had to skip back to the beginning of the song to start it over
to take it all in and make sure I didn't miss anything. While
listening to the entire verse, I scanned the car and sat in awe
of how it looked inside. Everything was plush and the CD
player screen flipped out with a push of a button. I noticed
the ashtray was cracked and the tail of a plastic baggie was
hanging out. I opened the ashtray and there was a large
sack of crack cocaine. I went to reach for it to see exactly
how much was in there and right before I touched it, I heard
two clicking noises and something cold pressed against my
right temple. "Get the fuck out my car nigga!" Scared as hell,
I turned towards him with my face staring at a .45 caliber
pistol.

With his right hand on the gun, he opened up the car door with his left hand and watched me very intently as I got out the car. As he shut the door I just stood there looking at him wondering if my curiosity would be the reason that I drew my last breath. He put his gun away after he heard Tasha's voice next to him telling him that I could be trusted, and I wouldn't steal from him.

He laughed at me and said, "Look at this scared ass nigga. I wasn't gon' do nothing to you nigga for real." Of course I didn't think the shit was funny and made it known to him once he put his gun away. After the air was clear and right before Shannon got into his car to leave I approached him. "What's up Shannon? Put me on with some work nigga so I can get in the game." Apparently he saw the eriousness in my eyes and told me to hop in his car and he would give me a ride home.

The short trip around the corner ended quickly with him parking. He paused for a few seconds and turned to me with a level of seriousness that I can still visualize. His words were cautionary and stern, "Listen nigga, I don't just go around trusting anybody. It's part of the rules of this shit. But something in my gut is telling me that you could be a down ass nigga, I see the hunger in your eyes. But understand this, the common downfall of people who get in the game is that they try to stay in it. The game is to be used, otherwise it uses you. Do what you gotta do to get over and get out, cause at the end of the day when you got it, nobody gives a shit what you did to get it.

If you rolling with me, ain't no room for snitching, I'm not down with that gang shit, know that my color is green and that's all I stand for. I'll introduce you to the game, but after that you will be on your own." I listened and took it all in and because I had been around the dope game for years, I thought it couldn't be that hard. Prior to even thinking about selling dope, I had done things that I still can't wrap my mind around. Aside from hustling and acting on impulse, I have no rationale that makes any sense to the adult me. I started out breaking into apartments during times when I was suspended from school.

I learned how to jimmy most patio doors open with a screwdriver and once in, I would steal anything that I could carry in broad daylight without looking like a thief. I would break into apartments where I lived when I knew the residents were out. Once inside, I looked for valuables and I'd even help myself to a bite to eat while I was there. That quick meal was usually a bowl of cereal and I'd leave the dirty bowl sitting on the counter as a calling card. At the time, I was into watching and reading about serial killers and I learned about little things they did that were consistent with each crime they committed.

For me, having a bowl of cereal and leaving the bowl on the counter was my MO. There also had been times I would eat and take a nap there because I was suspended and I could not stay home knowing that my mom was there. This left me with nowhere to go and I didn't want to just roam the streets. Once school was out, I would resurface and stay close by to watch the people come home and eventually the police would arrive. Once during my breaking and entering spree, the police were at an apartment that I had broken into earlier that day, and as I walked by the police I arrogantly asked what happened.

My mom ended up catching me one day while walking the streets during school hours with a bag full of things that I had just stolen from an apartment. She asked me why I was not in school, and after learning that I had stolen the valuables, she took them from me. I later found out that she had pawned those things and used the money for drugs. It got to the point where she soon knew I was stealing items and she would pawn or sell them, and only give me a small fraction of the profit. The most memorable break-in came one day when I broke into the apartment where a kid lived who went to my school.

Once I entered I began to search for jewelry and small valuables. As I walked up the stairs to the bedrooms, I looked into one room and noticed the boy from my school sleeping. My heart started to pound with anxiety and fear, as this had never happened to me before. I peeked into his parent's room and noticed the jewelry box sitting there wide open. I slowly walked across the hall and very quietly picked through things that I wanted and placed them in my book bag. As I walked past his room to head back down the stairs, I looked into his room to check on him. I noticed on his nightstand was cold medicine and additional items that let me know he was home sick.

I slowly started to walk down the stairs and about halfway down I stepped on the stair that made the loudest creaking noise I had ever heard. I then immediately heard movement from upstairs. I had to think quickly so I jumped down the remaining steps and ran back out the kitchen area where the patio door was located. It's when you're scared as hell that you typically run your fastest, and that was the only reason why I made it out of there without him seeing me. During that short time period, I had broken into over fifteen apartments. It wasn't too long before it caught up with me and I was questioned.

Detectives came to my mother's apartment one day after school asking a ton of questions. My mom lied and told them that during school hours when I was suspended, I was either home with her, or over a relative's house. After that day, I stopped breaking into apartments. It was soon after when I noticed that police cruisers were patrolling the apartments more often. Entering the dope game was a whole new adventure for me. Although I had been exposed to it, I actually knew nothing and Shannon treated me as such. He would ask me to give him whatever money I had and if I rolled with him, by the end of the day he would double my money, no questions asked.

Reluctant to just hand over all of my money, one Friday I decided to only give him $100 of the $150 I was holding. We then drove to the spot where he bought his crack and then set out on the highway to a small rural town called Coshocton, Ohio. He told me to use an alias when introducing myself to people in this town, and I became Anthony "Ant" Williams. Once we reached city limits, his pager would go off multiple times and every few miles resulted in stopping at payphones to return the phone calls of demanding customers.

After a few small word exchanges, we would make our rounds to houses one by one dropping off the dope, getting the money, and then on to the next stop. Sometimes we would end up back at the same house multiple times. My job was to deliver the product to them and return the money while Shannon waited in the car. By the end of the day, or early the next day, we would be on the road headed back to Columbus and as promised, my money had doubled. This process repeated itself multiple weekends in a row and as my trust with Shannon grew, I provided him with more money.

One weekend I had given him $500 that I earned at my third shift job at Denny's Restaurant as a busboy. I looked forward to those trips with Shannon, all the while watching my money stack up. The more money I got, the more I spent on clothes, jewelry, and anything else that I wanted. My girlfriend at the time could have just about anything she wanted. One day on one of those trips, Shannon noticed that I went out and bought yet another ring for my finger. He shook his head and simply asked me, "What you out here hustling for man? Like, what's your ultimate goal?" Confused, I offered no answer. He told me that I was a backwards hustler, and although I looked good, I had nothing of substance to show for my hustling and no money saved.

"Don't you notice I don't drive my nice car on these trips, I'm not flashy with clothes, or anything? When I go on these trips, it's about business and I'm not trying to stand out or draw any attention to myself." "You don't even have a fucking car to drive, depending on me to take you everywhere unless you decide to take the bus. You really need to get your priorities straight my nigga. I'm just about out the game after this summer, headed to Cincinnati for school. I'm not going to carry you anymore. It's time for you to branch out and hustle on your own. You can have a few of my loyal customers that you can reach out to if you just trying to double your money."

I took the lesson and words to heart, and it was after that conversation that he explained to me even more about the game that I just simply hadn't realized. The money I was giving him was actually putting more in his pockets even though we were doubling my money. Although the drugs were the same, the price would almost triple in those small cities and rural towns because of the limited access. So overall, the money I provided was giving him the ability to make an initial investment and purchase the drugs upfront, then he ended up making more than he gave me back.

I realized that he had made thousands of dollars off of me. I couldn't even be mad at him. From the weekend we spent, I became familiar with the Coshocton area and other surrounding cities myself. I used other people's cars to take the trip, and I had established a little clientele in cities there for myself. I would come in town, make my rounds, and was headed back to Columbus before the sun came up. The trips going to those cities were always a risk considering that I was a black male traveling to cities that were 99% white. Money was coming in regularly and rent was no longer an issue. I stacked my money like I was told and had so much that I resorted to hiding it all throughout my apartment for safekeeping.

I was never taught how to open up a bank account, so that wasn't an option for me. It was easy money and I wanted more. There were a couple of local dope boys that sold drugs in the Coshocton as well and they despised Shannon and me because they knew we were coming in at will and taking money they thought was rightfully theirs. One weekend, Shannon shared that one of the guys would be walking around with at least $3,000 in his pockets and suggested that I should rob him. His rationale was that he couldn't do it because he had family that lived in the city and they knew him too well.

He said that if I were successful in doing so, that I needed to give him one thousand of the three thousand for providing the lead. I took him up on his offer, knowing the dude wouldn't have a gun in his possession. Shannon provided me with the details on where he was going to be and the exact time that he would be walking out of the house with the money. I thought very long and hard about how to best pull this off without any problems and once I had a blueprint for my come up, I was ready and there was no turning back.

The time arrived and I proceeded with the plan. I was so sure I'd be successful that I had already envisioned buying a car with my winnings, which made my desire and motivation that much greater. The picture was already painted: I'd be rolling around with some rims and a booming system. At about 9:00pm just as Shannon had indicated, I saw the dude walking down the street. He had seen me before many times in the city so he knew who I was. I approached him with a friendly greeting and before he could get into his car, I pulled my .45, pointed it to his head, and instructed him to place his hands on the car. I told him if he moved I was going to blow his fucking head off.

As he placed both hands on the hood of his car, I ran his pockets and took wads of cash from each. I took his car keys and threw them deep in the bushes, then told him to take his shoes and pants off. Inside of his sock was also a bag of crack, which I also took. I made him not only lie on the ground, but I also had him slide under his car face down. I was calculated and didn't want him to know which direction I was heading. Once he did it I ran off with his clothes in my hand and ditched them in a trashcan once I was out of sight. Shannon was waiting a few blocks over with the car running. Adrenaline and nervousness were evident as I could hardly open the door before yelling, "Get me the fuck out of this city and take me home!"

As Shannon drove off I pulled out the money, heart still racing, sweat dripping from my face, and hands shaking. I immediately counted the money out and gave Shannon his cut. It seemed like the drive was taking hours to get back to Columbus. Once he dropped me off at my apartment, I entered to see my girlfriend who had been waiting on me. She could tell by the look in my eyes and unsettled nerves that I had done something, but I wasn't talking. Without her knowing, I walked to the closet pulled out a shoebox and emptied all of the loot from my pockets.

I laid it next to another shoebox I had which was also filled with money. The next day, word of my stick-up had made its way around the city and Shannon told me that I could never go back there again. I understood why, after all, I had robbed another guy who was attempting to do what I was being successful at and if the shoe were on the other foot, I'd be out looking for payback. Even though I understood, I needed to make one last trip to collect fifteen hundred dollars owed to me by one of my customers.

He advised against it but I decided after a few weeks that things should be settled and we set out on the road as we normally did. After I picked up my money, Shannon said that he needed to make one more stop and he would get back on the road. As we drove through the city I grew more paranoid with each minute that passed. We approached our destination and I walked in behind Shannon and sat in the living room waiting on him to finish his business in the kitchen. Time started to get away from us and my paranoia was heightened, so I walked into the kitchen and gave him a look that we often exchanged that meant it was time to leave.

I stood trying to mask my impatience as Shannon cut a piece of crack and passed it to the fiend. As the exchange was being made, someone knocked on the door. At that moment, my paranoia seemed to be justified because before we could find out who was at the door, a thunderous boom caused it to fly open. Instinct kicked in for me and as I was able to make out that someone had just kicked the door down, I was ducking for cover. Two gunshots rang out and I could hear the bullets travel in my direction and hit the wall next to my head.

Once I made my way behind another wall, the room fell silent and without hesitation, I reached into my waistband and retrieved my gun. I turned the corner and let off three shots of my own in the direction of the door. My shots caused whoever it was to flee and as I stepped around the corner to pursue I could see the dude I had robbed and stripped as he ran outside and passed the kitchen window. When our eyes met he raised his gun in my direction and I again let off three shots BLOWWWW, BLOWWWWWW, BLOWWWWW! I wasn't sure if he was hit or not because the shattering and flying glass was all that I remember seeing as he ran off. Shannon ran out the front door and I ran out behind him.

Once in the front yard, two more shots were fired in my direction and one hit the car in front of me. I jumped into Shannon's car and we sped off. The gun was too hot to place back in my waistband, so I stuck it under my seat. Just as soon as it had started, it was over but my heart still pounded. I was so scared I had to make sure that I wasn't shot and that I hadn't pissed my pants. Fortunately, neither had occurred. "I told your dumb ass not to come back to this city," Shannon screamed.

His words were followed by him rolling down his window and throwing out his gun and the dope he had in his pocket. He advised me to do the same but before I could, the police were behind us and within seconds their lights came on. With guns drawn, I soon stared down the barrel of a gun and one officer turned into twenty. We were completely surrounded. We both did as we were instructed and put our hands out of the windows. In no time flat we were both lying face down in the street.

Once handcuffed, we were placed in separate cars as they searched the vehicle. Shannon looked in my direction and shook his head. I read his lips as he said the words, "No snitching." We were both taken to police headquarters where we were questioned individually. The question they kept asking me was, "Who fired the shots?" I refused to say it was me and I refused to give up the name of the person that was firing the shots. After being advised that they would run a gunshot residue test, I felt like I was out of options. I soon broke down and told them that it was me that fired the shots, but only in self- defense.

I told them that I had no idea as to why I was being targeted, nor did I give up the name of the other shooter. They questioned me about Shannon selling drugs but I said nothing to incriminate him. In fact, I told them that I'd never known him to sell drugs and that he was on his way to college soon. I have no idea how or why I made it out that police station but after a few hours in the holding tank, they let us go with no charges.

They returned the money I had on me along with my other possessions and told me to never come back to their city again. And this time, I took heed to that warning. A few months later I learned that they had filed charges on the guy that fired the shots at me. I was summoned to court but I refused to cooperate. Unfortunately, I learned what it felt like to have my life flash before my eyes, how to stay tight-lipped, and the power of guardian angels all in the same day. I told the courts that I could not remember that evening and as I sat there on the witness stand looking at the guy who tried to take my life, I told the court that I didn't recognize him and that I'd never seen him before in my life.

Even today, I have no idea of what he was charged with or what the outcome was. I cut all ties with that city, changed my pager number, and never had communication with anyone from that place again. I had an experience that showed me really quickly the price one must be willing to pay in order to be heavy in the game. Death or incarceration was inevitable for those who sold dope, and it was clear that I wasn't ready to pay that price. After the dust settled, I went out and bought a car. I walked right onto the lot of a "buy here, pay here" dealership and paid cash for a 1990 Oldsmobile Ninety-Eight.

As I pulled out the wads of hundred dollar bills held together with rubber bands, I counted out the money to the dealer. He nodded his head as I counted and gave a slight smile that indicated he knew exactly how I got the money, but he asked no questions. In less than fifteen minutes, I sat in that car, adjusted my seat and proudly drove it off the lot. That same day, I stuck to my plan and tricked it out with a Pioneer CD player, two Road Thunder MTX 12-inch speakers, and a Rockford Fossgate 1000watt amp. Now I was making a statement. Every man has his weaknesses. I mean, it's the nature of the beast.

For some men it's a drug and the high associated with it, and they spend all of their time trying to recreate the first one. For others, it's the comfort of a beautiful woman that keeps them jonesin', even though that jones is the venom of the predator.

For some, it's the allure of money and the power that comes from having it. It's an old inevitability and no one is exempt, no matter what we would like to believe. Every one of us is susceptible to that one thing for which we will do almost anything. I've been on the exception of this affair, and at a very young age, I had the mentality that I would not be denied of my one tireless obsession. From as early as I can remember it was always about that dollar, and for years it had been that lover that kept me coming back for more.

The very first time I had her to call my own was at the age of twelve, and that's when I realized the power she had over me. She laid into me so tough, the ecstasy she gave became my very own personal utopia. No matter how much of her I had, I always found myself wanting more. Through all of my formative years money, both having it and not having it, ruled my actions. It caused me to do things that I'm very ashamed of and for which I have a great deal of remorse. In hindsight, I realize that it was my obsession for my timeless lover that made parts of my past a living hell.

I didn't realize it then, but it was a very one-sided relationship. I did for her, but she never did for me. I was willing to sacrifice my life for her, but she'd never do for me unless I did for her. She really cared nothing about me, and she knew that I knew it. I'm sure if she were real she would have sat back and laughed at the fool I had become for her. The things that I've shared isn't necessarily the tip of the iceberg, nor is it the muddled mass of ice that sank the Titanic.

It's more like the shadow in the water that lets you know that danger always lies ahead if you aren't careful about which way to go. My problem was that just like the Titanic, I never paid attention to any of the signs and chose not to change my course. I plowed on full speed ahead, believing that I was invincible. Unlike many folks who have hood tales to tell of hustling and being in the game, mine aren't intended to glorify my actions, but rather to paint a complete picture of who I was and what I did in comparison to who I am and what I'm doing.

"The streets don't love you, it just takes you away from the people who do" ~Rayshawn

COUNTY BLUES

Those who chose or were led to live lives of crime tend to recall an air of invincibility that clouded their vision while participating in activity that led to them being caught and eventually having some level of interaction with our country's criminal justice system. I am no exception. Never in a million years would I have thought that I would wind up prison. Even during the times when I was in the streets hustling trying to make a dollar and doing things I knew could lead to being locked up, the thought of having on those cold steel bracelets and sitting down for a little while didn't cross my mind.

The idea or thought of prison rarely, if ever, becomes real in a criminal's mind until the moment that all of the illegal activity comes to a head. Sometimes it's almost being caught, sometimes it's almost losing your life, and sometimes it happens once you've been caught. That realization is instantly sobering. You realize that there are consequences for every action. Some even spend those sobering moments trying to pinpoint the exact moment or action that lead to the epiphany; not for the sake of a moment of further enlightenment, but for the sake of not getting caught or having another close call again.

My incarceration ensued from a strange turn of events and an ironic twist of fate that to this day both troubles me, and demonstrates that God is in control and has a plan for us all. I'll be the first to disclose that while growing up and navigating my way through a sea of violence, I did a lot of things that were against the laws of man in order to keep my ship afloat. The irony stems from me knowing and being fully aware of all the ways that I had broken the law and never gotten caught (except for that one time in the grocery store), to eventually being incarcerated for a crime that I didn't commit, had no clue even occurred, and was not even in my hustler's repertoire.

It would take two years after my release for me to realize that God has a way of balancing life's scales and holding us accountable for what we do and don't do in this world. An algebra equation has to balance, and all of the necessary steps have to be completed in order for it to be solved. My story is no different. The how and why wouldn't be clear until after the necessary steps were completed in the equation. The prison experience in and of itself was a very horrifying one, one that I'd never wish on my worst enemy. However, it was an experience that truly turned my life around and put me on the path that would take me on my own personal journey to manhood.

Anyone who has ever been locked up has a different story to tell about his or her incarceration. The outcome, the effect, and the perspective are as uniquely different as rocks in an alley. One thing that is consistent is that no matter who you are or your perspective, the memories of your sentencing never fade. The closing of the gates behind you continue to echo in your mind long after the noise has dissipated.

The day was Tuesday, October 31, 1995, and I had just gotten off from working the third shift at Denny's as a bus boy. With no transportation that morning, I was able to catch a ride to my studio apartment about a mile from where I worked. Normally I would have just walked home, but two girls who were waitresses and happened to be roommates were nice enough to swing me by my place so that I could change, and then drive me to the courthouse so that I could pay an outstanding traffic ticket.

I was given a traffic ticket for driving without a license and the last thing I needed was to allow that ticket to be the reason my troubles persisted. The unwritten rule for food service industry workers states that when you leave work, the first thing you do is remove any reminders of work: uniforms, hats, name tags, and even the smell. In my opinion, the smell that clung to my white shirt and black *Dickies* slacks was almost sickening. It didn't help that smelling myself made me think of the grease trap, and Denny's did not pay me enough to deal with that smell on my own time.

Working there was simply a cover up to the hustling that I was doing. Smelling like an eight hour shift in that greasy dirty kitchen, I rushed into my apartment to change clothes before heading downtown. Upon entering my apartment I noticed that the door was unlocked. This was strange and a little eerie because I always made sure to lock my doors. I just didn't make those kinds of mistakes. If by chance I did make such a mistake, it wouldn't be at a time when I had an illegal handgun in my place and cash from selling crack.

A partner of mine decided to seize the moment when we saw a couple of unsuspecting rookies flossing their bankrolls at the mall. I waited for him to exit the mall and while donning ski masks, his money instantly became my money. It was easy and something we had done a time or two before. If you were foolish enough to try and show off your money or jewelry around me, I was hungry enough to take it. As I entered my apartment I noticed the place had been ransacked. My bed was turned over, all of my belongings were scattered on the floor, and it looked as if a windstorm had picked up everything and dumped it out of its proper place.

I immediately went to my stash spot in the back of the closet and my heart dropped when I realized that both the money and my gun were gone. With no time to ponder over the belongings, I went on to change my clothes and thought that I would just worry about it once I got back. What would I do, call the police to tell them I was robbed of some cash that I had from selling crack, or by recently robbing a man? Would I also mention the gun that had its serial numbers filed off of it? It pissed me off and I was a little worried, but the law of the streets was easy come, easy go.

As I ran out the door not wanting to keep my ride waiting too much longer, I became overcome by a feeling that led me to believe that today was not going to be a good day. The whole way to the courthouse I sat in thoughtful silence trying to figure out who would rob me. My first thought took me to my partner in crime. Even though we were cool, he ultimately could not be trusted.

He knew my work schedule as well as the exact location of where I stashed my gun and the cash. I made it a practice to hide money in my apartment in unsuspecting places like under the base of a lamp, in a food box in the freezer, and in my closet. This was one of those times I wished that I had been more selective with my hiding spot. I got out of the car once we arrived downtown, thanked the ladies for the ride, dropped them a few dollars for gas, and made my way to the courthouse. Once I was inside, I made my way to the floor for traffic court and had my name added to the day's docket to see the judge.

My first stop along the way was at the clerk's window. I gave the lady my name and social security number, and after about two minutes of typing in information, I saw a look go across her face that brought back the feeling I had about how my day was going to go. I asked her if there was a problem. She hesitated for a moment and asked me for my information again, which I then repeated. After reading over some information on the screen, she turned to me and said, "Do you know you have a warrant for your arrest on two counts of aggravated robbery, and one count of felonious assault?"

I looked at her like she was crazy and said, "No, I think there must be some mistake. There is no way that I would be charged with such a thing." She leaned over the counter and told me to wait, and that she would be back in a second. My first instinct was to break camp and get the hell out of there as fast as I could, but that thought soon passed. Only guilty people run, and deep in my heart I knew there was no way that they were really looking for me. In regards to the crime they were referring to, I was innocent.

I thought back to all the dirt I had done that summer, and none of the charges she shared made any sense. Time passed and it seemed like an hour until she returned with papers in her hand for me to read. She stated that she wasn't supposed to let me read the complaint, but because of the seriousness of the charges, she was inclined to bend the rules. As I began to read the complaint, the feeling that I got in my stomach grew more intense.

On July 19, 1995, I was accused of robbing and stabbing a white man at a Swifty gas station on Morse Road. I remember thinking "Damn, that's way up North!" The warrant had just been issued the night before, and now I thought about the police possibly being the ones who had been in my apartment. After reading the complaint, the feeling in my stomach turned to a fear that was so tangible, I could have passed it out to the folks passing by. I wanted to cry but I held back the tears in front of not only the lady that was helping me, but from the ten other people that were behind me listening to the whole conversation.

I politely handed her back the complaint and told her that I had done no such thing and had no idea what this was all about. She told me that she was not going to call the police, and if I still wanted to be on the docket I could. But more than likely, they would take me to jail, and the police were going to catch me sooner or later if I didn't turn myself in. Not being the most legally savvy young hustler, I persisted and asked her to put me on the docket. I thought that once I had an opportunity to explain myself that everything would be cool, and I would be home soon.

She gave me the courtroom number, and I proceeded to make my way downstairs still having a very real fear in my heart and that strange feeling in my stomach. At eighteen, and like most other people who have their first brush with the law, oblivion exists, and that day not only did oblivion exist, but I was under the impression that I was still considered a juvenile. Just one month prior, I was arrested for receiving stolen property, and the bond of $250 was paid by a mentor. I had not yet learned the outcome of those charges, and even with that situation I thought that beating the charge was inevitable.

I made my way into the courtroom and took a seat close to the rear of the gallery in case I had second thoughts and decided to walk out. I wouldn't be noticed and disappearing would be easy. Case by case I listened as each individual's name was called, and their time in front of the judge included him issuing harsh fines for misdemeanor offenses. About an hour into the caseload I heard a man call my name. Although I was waiting to hear my name, it still caught me off guard. I immediately stood to my feet and walked forward in seemingly slow motion. As I continued my pace, I noticed two court officials talking to one another.

One of the men held my file in one hand, and what I would soon learn was a warrant for my arrest in the other. As each slow step took me closer to the center of the courtroom, a sheriff's deputy entered the courtroom from the same door I was sure to sit next to. The other official and party to the covert conversation pointed me out to the deputy as if to say in a whisper, "Yep, that's him right there." I approached the table and the prosecutor asked me to state my name and social security number. I was soon led behind the same doors that I saw the second sheriff enter from, and immediately I burst into tears. I was read my rights and handcuffed.

At that very moment, I thought that my life had ended, that nothing else mattered. He told me what I was charged with then ushered me to booking. Once inside the booking room, I was placed in a holding cell with five other black men who were waiting to be processed as well. As the loud clank of the steel doors ensured that they had just closed behind me, I found it impossible to sit. All I could do was stand there with tears streaming down my face. I had no idea of what had just happened. The men in the room grew tired of me crying and one offered some brand of twisted encouragement, "Damn nigga, if you didn't kill nobody can you shut the fuck up?"

The other four erupted in laughter and even though I didn't think shit was funny, I began to pull myself together. Trying to stop crying proved to be a difficult task with my short and choppy breaths, and I was taken back to childhood whoopings that were almost always followed by a deep sleep and a renewed chance at childhood upon waking up. I could only hope for one of those naps now. I would have even traded any of those embarrassing childhood moments for my current predicament. Before long, it was my turn to be stripped, searched, and tossed a pair of stiff rough pants and short-sleeve shirt I'd come to know as county blues. I could tell by the way the pants almost stood by themselves that they were strangers to the fabric softener sheets that my mother would use, and the shirt wasn't my size no matter what the tag said. A bright orange bracelet that served to alert jail officials that I was being charged with a felony followed the blues.

The white bracelets indicated misdemeanor cases, and the bright yellow was for federal offenses. Federal time was said to be the hardest time a man could serve. It didn't take long before the last little bit of pride I had was gone. Stripped down to "ass holes and toes" in front of complete strangers not only made me think about all the horror stories I'd heard about men being raped in jails and prison, but it also made me feel like more of an animal and less of a man. I had just become someone's property, and powerless against imposing my own will.

I hesitated at first, but the officer on duty insisted that I put a rush on it. He made it clear that he had ten other people to get processed and I was holding up the show. While changing into my "county blues" and packing up personal belongings, he began to yell out the rules. In between telling us where to, how to, and what not to, he and the staff began handing out items. The instructions bounced off the cold brick walls and echoed in my ears until the next words hurried them along much like we were being. I was given a hard plastic drinking cup, a tube of toothpaste that was labeled "Tooth Paste," a black plastic comb that reminded me of picture day in elementary school, and a pair of cheap brown plastic slippers.

I couldn't help to think that picture day at school would have been a much better place to be. We were given a mat to sleep on that was as hard as the plastic slippers I had just slid onto my feet and just as thin as the soles. The sheet and coarse wool blanket didn't promise a comfortable or warm night's sleep either. I was nearly the last person to get my only phone call, and the only person that I had to call at that time was my girlfriend. I had no idea what her reaction would be to my telling her that I was in jail. She was on full academic scholarship at The Ohio State University and living in the college residence halls. She had been down for me almost a year, and had my back just as much as I had hers.

The only woman that was willing to accept me, love me, and even hustle with me and for me. I loved her for it. In order to reach her, I would have to call her parents' house because the phones in the college dorms did not accept collect calls. As the phone rang, I had no idea how I would even explain it to her mom, who by then really didn't care too much for me. I had made Tiffany move in with me for the most part of that summer because she was always arguing at home with her mom and sister, and I couldn't take it anymore just as much as she couldn't. When the call connected, immediately I could tell that she was not pleased to be hearing from me. I explained what happened, the charges that were against me, and asked her to put me on 3-way to call Tiffany.

She agreed, and as I was placed on hold, my heart began to sink with sadness. After two rings, Tiffany picked up the phone and her mom explained to her that I was on the phone via 3- way. After taking a long pause I explained to her what I was charged with, and immediately I heard the sobbing and the tears through the phone. It had always been gut-wrenching for me to see a woman that I loved in pain. Each sob hurt more than the previous and although I was accustomed to seeing my mother hurt and experiencing pain and strife, the feeling of helplessness never subsided. Helplessness and fear began to overcome me and my tears began to flow again, and as they flowed, I tried to assure her (and myself) that things were going to be okay. In between deep gasps and wiping my face I assured her that I hadn't done what I was accused of doing.

Before too long, I heard the sheriff in the background telling me that my time was up. I ended the phone conversation with her like I always did, by saying I love you. I was soon led upstairs to the 8th floor West Unit where an eight-man cell awaited me. As the sheriff's deputy shuffled from key to key on a massive key ring, I could hear noise and yelling coming from the very place that I was soon going to enter. I could feel fear and anxiety churning in my stomach, and it was all I could do to breathe and prevent that fear from spilling out of my mouth and onto the floor.

With what little time I had left, I wiped away any evidence of tears, and braced myself for the unexpected. As the cell door opened and I walked in, I noticed two beds were free. Before I could choose one, the cell slammed shut and the echo and hollow traveled from my ears, down my spine to the soles of my feet. After catching a few mean mugs and cold stares from the other inmates, most went back to what they were doing. I approached the bottom bunk closest to the door and began to unroll my mat and fit it with the sheets and blanket. After getting myself settled, I laid on my bunk and once again pulled out the complaint papers.

I read them almost to the point of memorizing each line with the hopes of finding a mistake that would set me free. Reading turned to delirium, and I soon feel asleep. I wished I could fall asleep and wake up from this horrible nightmare. Well into my sleep induced escape, I was jolted back into reality by a loud mouth officer screaming, "Rayshawn Wilson get up, you got a visitor!" Immediately I jumped to my feet curious to see who was here to see me, and hopefully set me free. As I made my way down the hall, I first thought it was Tiffany, but we soon walked right past the visiting booths.

I was led into a waiting elevator where another officer was waiting to escort me. Once the door opened, I was back on the first floor then led into a conference room where an average sized white man, whom I had never seen before, was waiting on me. The man, dressed in a shirt and tie, looked to be in his early 40s. I remember feeling like the visit wouldn't be good when I saw how ugly the tie was that he wore. Eager and ready to get some answers, without a request to do so, I rushed to pull a chair and took a seat. He introduced himself as Detective Stone, the officer Investigating the crime in which I was being charged.

All that separated him and I was the cold brown table and a black tape recorder. He read me my rights and got right to work by pushing the "record" button on the tape recorder. He first asked me where I was late last night and shared that they had been looking for me. I explained to him that I was working the third shift at Denny's and I didn't get home until my shift ended. He looked at me and without saying the words, I could see that he thought I was lying.

"Now tell me where you really were," soon followed the light chuckle that flowed from his mouth. I asked him if they were the ones responsible for breaking into my apartment, and he replied that he had no idea what I was talking about. He then asked me where I was on the night of July 19, 1995, at around 10:00pm. I replied by stating that it was over two months ago and that he couldn't possibly expect me to remember where I was at that time. The one thing I did know was that I damn sure wasn't out robbing or stabbing anyone.

He then pulled out a composite sketch in black and white. The picture was supposed to look like me, but there was no resemblance. The sketch was of a man with light facial hair and a ball cap on his head with the brim of the cap flipped up in the front. I began to point out obvious differences between this picture and me: I didn't own or wear baseball caps, and I had no facial hair because mine had not yet begun to grow. He slid the picture across the table to me and asked, "Take a look at this picture, don't this look like you?" I said no with as much hostility as I could. All of a sudden I could sense his frustration and his face began to turn red.

He then pulled out a photo lineup containing five other men and myself. Each of us were young and African-American. I recognized the picture of me because it was taken after a previous charge for receiving stolen property. There was one difference from my picture and the rest of them: mine had a circle around it with the letters "SB" beside it. While looking at the rest of the people in the lineup, I noticed three guys I once hung out with in the projects and other surrounding areas.

One of them was a picture of Kenny that used to bully me while living in the projects back in the day. Although I felt pretty doomed and unlucky that day, I must admit that fate has truly been on my side since the three guys I recognized never made it to the age of thirty. All three were dead at the hands of a gunman.

While still red in the face, yet smirking like he was about to win, he looked at me and said, "In all of my years of doing this, I've never seen a victim point a guy out in less than ten seconds and start crying." While he was saying that, he was also packing up his belongings as if he was done with me. My frustration wouldn't allow me to turn red but I expressed it. I told him that I had nothing to do with this shit and threw the lineup back his way.

He stopped the tape recorder, told me to have a goodnight, and to "explain that sob ass story to the judge." Angered, and even more frustrated as I headed back to my cell, I had no idea what to expect from there, or how to prove that I was innocent. The next morning I went in front of a judge, and for reasons that only God knows, I thought that I was going to get in front of this man, proclaim my innocence, and be let me go.

I pled not guilty to all of the charges, and was hit with a $150,000 bond on the robbery case, and a $50,000 bond for the RSP case. The whole proceeding took less than two minutes. Just as quickly as they had called my name to enter, I was being herded back to the holding cell where I would wait to be escorted back to my floor. The high bond only ensured that I wouldn't get out, and I knew that after figuring what ten percent of $200,000 was. No one I knew had that kind of money, and if they had property as collateral, they damn sure weren't putting it up for me.

After talking to some fellow inmates, it didn't take long for me to realize how serious my situation was. In the days to come I was assigned a public defender that was going to be handling my case. I placed a collect call to the Public Defender's office prior to knowing who my lawyer would be, and I was told that I had one of the best public defenders in the city. It was also communicated to me that Scott Wiseman had a pretty good track record with handling charges like mine.

He stood about 5'9" with a football player's build, baldhead, and unlike the detective with the ugly tie, he dressed really nice. He informed me that we had a really good chance of beating the robbery case, but if I did, the prosecutors would be upset and attempt to give me jail time for the RSP. If I was found guilty of the robbery charges, I was facing 10-25 years.

The mere thought of facing that much time made me sick to my stomach, and I thought about being at least thirty years of age before I even went to the parole board. The evidence against me was simple: supposedly, someone called crime stoppers and gave them my name. Soon after, I was picked out of a picture photo array line up. I was also told that there had been two black males fleeing the scene of a crime and heading in an unknown direction.
Because I couldn't remember my whereabouts and activity for that day, I had no alibi. After the initial meeting with Scott, I placed a collect call to Tiffany to give her an update. To my surprise, she was able to help me remember that exact day. She told me that was her older sister's birthday and she remembered the day very well. Acco rding to her, that was the day I was at my apartment studying to take the Ohio ninth grade proficiency test, which I was scheduled to take the very next day at East High school. She was there with me the whole night, and not once did I leave my apartment. Records confirmed that I in fact did take the test that next day. As directed, I immediately let my public defender know that I now had an alibi and that I was able to remember where I was on the day in question.

In the days to come, I remained in the Franklin county jail as more information came my way regarding the case. My public defender filed a motion of discovery, which meant I was to be given all of the evidence that was being used against me, as well as any other important information. I remember getting the package in the mail during mail call and couldn't wait to open it. While reviewing the contents of the package, I came across the victim's personal information like house address and phone number, and the medical information from his hospital visit. One thing I instantly noticed from the reports was the mention that he was under the influence of marijuana at the time of the robbery. In my mind, this was something that should work in my favor. How could he have accurately picked me out if he was high when the crime was committed?

I also came across his telephone number and everything in me wanted to call this guy in order to get an understanding of what happened that night. I took the papers over to the telephones and began to think, "The worst that could happen is that he not accept the collect call." Nervously, I dialed the number and when it was time for me to say my name I simply said, "This call is for Steve Blackwell." While being placed on hold to see if the collect call would be accepted, I contemplated hanging up. But sooner than those thoughts came to my mind, the call was accepted and he was on the phone.

Since it all happened so fast, I hadn't considered my approach, but instinct cleared the way for rage. I was being accused and jailed for something I did not do, and now was my chance to let the accuser know that he had the wrong guy. Instead, in a soft calm voice I introduced myself and told him that I was sorry for calling him like this, but I wanted to talk to him about the crime that took place.
I asked him how he was so certain that I was the one that did that to him. He assured me that he knew it was me unless I had a twin.

He also said that he wished I wouldn't have stabbed him and just took the gas station money. I pleaded with him that I was not the one who had hurt him, and begged him to reconsider. He said that it was "out of his hands, sorry for my luck" and he "hoped that I would learn from my mistake." Before I could say anything else to convince him that he was wrong, the phone went dead and he was gone. I dropped the phone and I stood there as the phone swung back and forth like the pendulum on a clock.

The familiar feelings of being lost in the world without anyone to turn to were my only company. Within hours of making that phone call, I was called out of the cell by one of the Sheriff Officers. He then led me to a different room where another officer was waiting. He sat me down and explained to me that calling the victim could result in additional charges. Apparently they had been listening to the call the entire time. I agreed that I would not contact him again.

Weeks passed with continuations and motions, and with each unanswered question and day that passed, I grew more impatient. Knowing that I didn't have any control over my life at that point was as empty of a feeling as I had ever felt, and not being able to defend myself contributed to thoughts that I was doomed. The environment, daily regimen, lack of privacy, and absence of freedom grew old. I became very agitated and everything around me only made it worse. I began to feel like a caged animal and the anxiety from worrying about my case was compounded by the fact that I shared space with eight other people who were also facing charges of violent crimes.

One guy was in for murder and claimed self-defense even though the victim was shot in the back. After reading his motion of discovery and other information pertaining to his case, I was shocked to read that prosecutors were seeking the death penalty. He shot a man with a 44-caliber handgun four times in the back after being robbed of some drugs that weren't even his. He had already been in the county for two years awaiting trail, and he danced his ass around that cell as if nothing was going on. Like his life was not hanging in the balance.

I wanted to ask him how he could always be in such a good mood knowing what he was up against but that would have come across as weak on my part. I knew from growing up in Lincoln Park Projects that weakness would not help me survive. Because I had been on my own and was no stranger to relationships with girls and women, I also grew sexually frustrated. I remember taking a nap and waking to a soaking wet crotch. I had no idea who the dream was about; I just remember wet dreams being a welcomed escape from the agony and chaos that seemed to follow me wherever I went.

Up until that point in my life, homosexuality was something that I had heard of, but never been exposed to. I had seen both men and women in various settings that you could tell were gay by their actions or style of dress, but prison was about to expose me to something that I was never prepared to see, and honestly wished I hadn't.

I awoke close to 5:00 am before breakfast to go to the restroom before the others got up and made it filthy. As I made my way to the toilet, which was in plain view of every bed in the area, I heard moaning and heavy breathing coming from around the corner. I slowly tiptoed closer to the noise and as I peeked around the corner, I saw Ramon (the guy who was charged with murder) with his pants down and another inmate bent over in front of him on the other side of the bars. I also recognized the guy who was bent over. He was a porter responsible for delivering items like mail and coffee to inmates. I stood there in partial disbelief and surprise by the determination of these two.

The men were having anal sex between prison bars and seemed to be enjoying themselves. At that moment I realized that my earlier question to Ramon about how he was able to walk around like jail was a nice place to be, was answered. I tipped back into my bed and acted as if I was asleep. I was saddened by the experience and swore that I wouldn't allow myself to become so comfortable with this place that I ever viewed that as normal. More importantly I'd never become either of those guys.

After that morning, every time I saw the porter walk by I would notice the exchange of a head nod between the two men. Although I made it my business not to get up that early again, what I witnessed between them wouldn't be my last viewing not only with them, but also with others.
The holidays were quickly approaching along with my nineteenth birthday, and I was finally given a trial date. My public defender insisted that we had a good case, and he also took comfort in knowing that whoever this mystery person was that called crime stoppers would have to come to court and testify.

Towards the end of December, about a week before my January 3rd court date, Tiffany dropped off some clothes for me so that I didn't have to walk in front of a jury wearing prison blues. As each day brought me closer to the trial, I started to grow more and more anxious. Just knowing that every word and action of mine was going to be evaluated and could affect my life from that point forward was more than I was prepared to handle.

Whether fully equipped or unprepared, it was inevitable. Somehow I was still able to find some confidence in knowing that once the jury heard what I had to say, I would be acquitted of the charges and move on with my life. The day of the trial arrived and I found myself sitting in a one- man cell awaiting my public defender. The time seemed to move slower than normal, and all I could think about was putting on my street clothes and walking into the courtroom with confidence and letting the facts set me free. The time came when my public defender approached my cell, but instead of clothes and a strategy for picking jurors, he shared that he had some "spur of the moment news" to share with me.

A conversation with the prosecutor revealed that she was willing to drop the two counts of aggravated robbery and felonious assault down to theft, which was a 5th degree felony. She stated that she would also drop the RSP down to a misdemeanor. If I was willing to accept the amended charges in the form of a plea deal, I would serve a total of two years in prison, and that my time already spent in the county jail would count towards my sentence. If I decided that I did not want to accept the deal, I could take it to trial. The risk I ran was the possibility that I could be found guilty and face the maximum punishment for the original charges. If I took the deal, after thirty days of receiving my inmate number, I could file for shock probation through the judge.

I had a good chance of getting it given that I was a first time offender. He also made mention that I could probably go through a boot camp program for ninety days and be sent to a halfway house for another thirty days and be on parole for a while. Simply put, I didn't know what to do. There were so many scenarios playing out in my mind, and none of them were the one that involved me walking away from this scot-free. Life had already taught me to stand up for myself and I couldn't imagine pleading guilty to something that I didn't do. I asked if I could have a few days to think about it. Scott looked at his watch and said, "Umm no, you have about 15 minutes to make a decision that I can provide to the prosecutor."

I then asked if there was a way that I could get probation and if he could go back out and talk to her again. He replied, "I'll see what I can do but I doubt if she is going to go any lower than what is being presented right now." As I sat there in the cold cell I realized there was no opportunity to talk it over with anyone who cared about me, or who was smarter than I was, or who had experience with the legal system. I had to make a decision that would affect me for the rest of my life within the next fifteen minutes. Once he left, other inmates that were waiting to go to court heard what was going on and I heard one of them say, "Man, you better take that deal and run with it. Don't be playing with them white folks like that."

No sooner than he said that, another guy next to me yelled, "Fuck that shit nigga! If you didn't do it, you take that shit straight to the box and make them prove that you did it." I stood with those voices in each ear and then time seemed to move faster than ever. Doubt, fear, anxiety and confusion were all too familiar emotions, but during those fifteen minutes, they were heavier as I held my head in my hand. There was no comfort, no peace. Through the weight of those fifteen minutes I remember thinking that being found guilty somehow and doing 10-25 years with no possibility of seeing the parole board until 2006 was like a death sentence for me.

That fact alone literally scared me to the point of needing to use the restroom. I couldn't take the risk of gambling and losing. I decided to take the deal. Once I gave my public defender my decision, I sat on the cold bench and wondered what I had just done. Confirmation that I wouldn't be going home made me nervous about the uncertainty of my future.

All the hope I had of being exonerated was gone in an instant. A feeling of sickness came over me and before I knew it, I was led in handcuffs by a sheriff's deputy into the courtroom. The paperwork was read and reviewed and I was asked to sign. At the stroke of that ink pen, I had just placed my life in the hands of the criminal justice system. Once the judge entered the room I stood there with a blank stare on my face, a churning in my stomach, and rapidly beating heart but I don't remember much else until the judge began to read the sentence.

He also asked if I had been promised any favors from anyone, and whether or not I was agreeing to the terms that were placed in front of me. My heart wouldn't allow me to speak so instead, I slowly shook my head in agreement. He then asked me if I had anything I would like to say about the situation. I paused and at that very moment, I wanted to recant my guilty plea. My brain told my mouth to begin speaking the words, "I didn't do it!" but my public defender leaned in. His advice came by way of a whisper in my ear, "Just say that you understand what is taking place."

On January 3, 1996, I was the first conviction of the New Year. "Rayshawn Wilson, I hereby sentence you to 24 months to be served within the Ohio Department of Rehabilitation and Corrections."

"Prison robs me of my dignity, my pride; it robs me of my privacy and of my freedom. Prison robs me of anything a man can enjoy in life."
~Rayshawn

325-675

After I was sentenced, I was moved from my regular cellblock and transferred to another where others were also waiting to be shipped out to the Correctional Reception Center (CRC). The reception center was a facility where new inmates were shipped to be classified and processed before being shipped off again to their permanent institution. The CRC is where psychological tests are administered, medical evaluations are conducted, and a man with a name becomes an inmate with a number. Due to security reasons, inmates are never told when they're leaving the county to head to CRC. Therefore, we all just sat and waited. When entering the sentencing tank one would think they just entered the zoo, or a big house party.

The cellblock was much bigger than the one I was previously in, holding sixteen or so inmates. After getting comfortable in my new bed, I laid there thinking about what was ahead of me. My initial hope was that I would get shock probation after thirty days of being in CRC. Getting to go to boot camp was second on my wish list. I also had to think about the possibility of maxing out and doing all of my time, which caused a sadness that I hadn't felt since not having a place to call home as a child. I overheard a guy mention that he was just sentenced to 25 years. I immediately rose up from my bed and noticed that the guy looked no older than myself.

Based on his body language, I sensed that not only was he mentioning it, but he appeared to be proud of his number. If my ass had been sentenced to 25 years, I don't think that I could have made it to the sentencing block. They would have been making funeral arrangements instead, because there's no doubt that at 19-years-old, I would have taken my own life. The mood and the atmosphere were very different in comparison to where I had previously come from.

The reality of years away from home, loved ones, and freedom were burdens that every man wore like an albatross. Phone calls to the outside about adding money to books were more regular than inmate count. Some inmates found a way to rig the phones in the cells that would allow incoming phone calls. When it was first brought to my attention, I didn't believe it until I was on a nearby phone and watched this guy in action. He picked up the phone and without dialing, started saying hello multiple times into the phone. After about 30 seconds he began having a conversation. I watched this scenario play out many times from different players in the cell.

They would have their loved ones call at a specific time, and then go to the phone and begin the, "hello, hello, hello" regiment until there was a voice on the other end. Like any other luxury from the outside world, I would soon learn that it if you wanted it, you had better be willing to pay for it. The price for incoming calls would vary from person to person, so it was like shopping for the best deal in town. I ended up buying the phone number from a guy that was in need of food. For thirty dollars worth of commissary, I was the proud owner of the incoming call number. For what it was worth, I only ended up staying in the sentencing block for a little over a week and again, for security reasons, you never knew when you were going to be shipped out. The morning that my name was called, I remembered being excited to begin my sentence, yet nervous and scared of the unexpected.

As I rolled up my belongings, I could hear people saying their good-byes. Some gave away items that they no longer needed or wouldn't be allowed to take with them. Those were the only times when anything was free on the inside. I was escorted back to the receiving unit where I was allowed to take off my county blues and put back on the clothing in which I had come. Putting those clothes on gave me a sense of false reality of what I was getting ready to face. My other personal belongings such as my pager, gold chain, and rings were sealed in an envelope and later shipped to a loved one.

One by one we were shackled together in pairs and led to a huge bus. After three months of brick walls, cells and inmates, it was such a relief to finally see the outside world once the bus left the garage. Highways, open fields, birds, the sky, people in cars all seemed like things I had taken for granted, but now appreciated seeing during that bus ride from Columbus to Orient. Upon entering the institution, I was stripped searched and thrown into a room with about 20 other buck naked men until they called my name.

Before the end of the day, I was given what would be my name for the next year and a half: Inmate #325-675. The realization that I was in prison did not settle in with me until I was in the chow hall for lunch. I saw an old partna' of mine that I went to middle school with when I was being escorted through the building, and without hesitation I yelled clear across the room to get his attention. A guy behind me pulled on my shirt and whispered to me that I was not allowed to do that. Out of excitement to see a familiar face, I didn't listen to him and I continued to yell across the room, even throwing my hands up in the air to get his attention.

Soon after, a white man came rushing over to me wearing a white shirt, which I would later understand were reserved for high- ranking correctional officers. His instructions were loud and to the point, "Shut the fuck up while you're in my line," and "This is not the time or place to be making small talk." In a show of disrespect for the lack of respect I was just given, I looked him up and down as if to say I would knock the shit out of him if the rest of the correctional officers weren't around.

Instead I turned around, faced the front and in my head mumbled, "This is some bullshit!" After getting my plate of food I sat down at a small table with about six other people and tried to make small talk with others. I realized that while I was talking, people were damn near inhaling their food. They knew something I didn't. Once I began to eat I was told (along with the rest of the men at my table) to stand up and throw my food away. I was trying to eat while I was walking to the trashcan but couldn't finish.

In total there were about five minutes from the time we entered the cafeteria to the time we were being escorted out, and the next group of inmates were herded in.
There would be no more talking for me when it was time to eat. While we were walking back to our pod, an old timer was behind me trying to school me on the ins and outs of prison life. He basically told me to keep my mouth shut, and that this was no place to be trying to act like a superhero. Once I got into my cell and those steel doors slammed shut behind me for the first time, I felt like a caged animal. I looked out the little square window only being able to see that other brick buildings and barbed wire fences along the perimeter surrounded me.

Not only was my vision limited to inside the fence, my thoughts were too. Eyes blurry from the flow of tears, I again cried myself to sleep, hoping to wake up in my apartment and realize that it had all been a nightmare. Of all the experiences and things that happened to me while I was locked up, I will never forget the first night. Sleeplessness caused me to lie awake with my thoughts. I began to think about all of the hustling and crimes I committed that never landed me in any trouble. Even after looking at it from that standpoint, it felt unfair that I was serving time for not only a crime I didn't commit, but one that was violent and resulted in someone physically being hurt.

The dream that came once I finally found sleep would change my outlook and attitude towards my prison experience and ultimately, my life. During my dream I could see myself at different phases of my life up to that point. The black and white bricks on the wall of my cell played out each act of mischief, crime, and all of my hustles. The episodes flashed from brick to brick as if each one was a television. The episodes didn't allow me to claim victory. In fact, they made me for once consider the impact my actions had on others. It was at that exact time that the dream began to haunt me.

I could feel the brick walls closing in on me. I began hearing screams and gunshots and in the midst of those noises in my head, the walls continued to close in on me. They appeared to be close enough on all four sides to touch and my tears began to roll. My tears and the fear were real, real enough for me to cry out "I'm sorry." My apology wasn't good enough, because the next vision I saw was the barrel of a gun. A voice followed and it asked me, "This is what you want, isn't it? This is the game that you wanted to play right? Look at me when I'm talking you! You want to continue to take chances and gamble with life? Then keep on doing what you're doing." Then I heard the hammer of the gun click as I watched the cylinder rotate.

By this point I was on my knees with a face full of tears, begging for forgiveness with my arms spread apart pleading for him not to kill him. All of a sudden another voice appeared and although it was from a further distance, it sounded even louder, "Come to me, follow the sound of my voice, and I'll comfort you and keep you safe from harm." Without even seeing the face, and with the gun still pointed at my head, I stood up and followed the sound of his voice. Then I heard the words, "Trust in the Lord with all your heart, and know that God has a better plan for you."

With my arms wide open I moved as if the cell would allow me to follow the voice I was hearing. Feeling as if I was right next to him I could clearly hear him say, "Follow the sound of my voice, I will always be by your side and I'll never put more on you than you can bear." As soon as I thought that I was next to the voice, it would fade away again, and then come back only to say, "Follow the sound of my voice." The comfort and peace I felt at that moment still lives in me, and whenever I feel challenged about anything, I recall that experience and call on God to provide His words and will to guide me.

While I was incarcerated at CRC I hit the 30-day mark, which meant I could file for shock probation. All I had to do was call my public defender and request that he file the paperwork for early release. I wrote to the judge asking for early release and detailed how the experience of the past couple of months had changed my outlook, and that I was ready to be released and live life as a productive citizen. It didn't take long after filing before the rejection came, for the nature of the crime made it easy for the judge to make the decision.

I was hoping that my lack of a record would have encouraged him to see things my way. To my disappointment, having no prior offenses did not seem to have any impact. My second option was to enter a boot camp program. As soon as I was over the disappointment of being denied shock probation, I was excited about boot camp. Needless to say that the cycle of excitement and disappointment was something I should have begun to get used to. I was quickly denied admission into the program. The idea was to enter boot camp for ninety days, then be released to a halfway house for thirty to sixty days before going on parole.

During that time I would be permitted to get my GED while participating in military style exercises. Those who refused to follow rules and stay in good standing while in boot camp were shipped up the hill to do their regular prison time. After a few weeks at CRC, it didn't take long before I was shipped to the prison on the hill, which was commonly referred to as "Gladiator Camp" because of its hostile atmosphere. Located in Lancaster, Ohio, the prison was once some sort of boys camp before being transformed into a penitentiary. I found irony in learning that, especially when I looked around and noticed that a lot of the inmates were my age.

After receiving my steel locker box filled with the basic necessities, I was given my dorm assignment and followed several other inmates down the yard to "I-Dorm." While walking down the sidewalk, I took some time to observe my surroundings. The bricks all seemed a little colder than bricks out in the free world and the prison resembled a small city, only caged in. It became clearer that I wasn't in a small city when we were greeted with verbal insults. They seemed to be coming from every window and the chorus of chaos was deafening. Each obscenity came through with crystal clear clarity and while I thought to myself, "They ain't talkin' to me," I was also instantly reminded that I did not want to be there. My resentment turned into confusion when what looked like a woman approached from a distance.

She wore a blouse tied in a knot right above her right pant pocket, hair in a ponytail, and red lipstick. She was short in stature, fair-skinned, and had a walk that demanded attention. As the line I was in processed through the yard, she began to bend over and was intent on us seeing the thong underwear she wore. A few of the men began to whistle and called her Tootie, and it was clear that attention was her goal. As we got closer to Tootie, my confusion turned to disgust.

I could see enough beard stubble and strong facial features to know that Tootie wasn't a woman, Tootie was a man. The blouse was a prison issued t-shirt, and I would later find out that the lipstick was powdered kool-aid drink mix mixed with Vaseline and his Hanes underwear were cut to resemble a woman's panties. Clearly someone in that place enjoyed the show, and based on my previous experience in the county, I know there was probably some guy who looked forward to alone time with Tootie, but I wasn't interested in any of that.

I soon entered I-Dorm which had been labeled one of the best dorms to be in on the yard. From the outside it looked more like a warehouse, and once inside a huge sitting area was the focal point. There were about five picnic tables and chairs scattered around one television. The sitting area led to the living quarters that reinforced the warehouse feel. There were over 200 bunk beds all lined in neat rows as far as my eyes could see. A corrections officer (or CO as we called them) was standing in the doorway and told us to find an empty bed then report back to him with the bed number.

Many of the inmates stopped what they were doing and watched us come in. I could tell they were looking to see which beds we picked. As I made my way down the first aisle, I saw a section that had three open slots. As I approached the first open bed I made my way around two inmates who didn't move or make it easy for me to access; they only offered cold stares. I gave them the nod that says, "What's up," and they looked and replied, "Naw man you can't have that bed, you gotta pick something else." I made my way down a little further, and soon noticed that the same two inmates followed me.

I started to set my belongings down in front of another bed and as soon as I tried I heard a voice behind me say, "Not that one either." I sat my things down anyhow, turned to face them and said, "Well why don't one of y'all niggas tell me where I can go then." I soon realized that I brought more attention to myself then I needed to, and another guy immediately rushed over and asked me who the fuck I was raising my voice at. Before I could get a word out I realized that I was surrounded by four people. I slowly and quietly picked up my box and moved on to another aisle.

After about five minutes I had found a bunk that seemed safe and didn't come with the musical chairs type of game. I was right by the door and close to the CO's table. There were over 200 or so inmates in this one dorm with only two CO's on duty at one time. After making my bed up, I climbed on the top and just looked around, taking in my surroundings. From where I lay, I had a clear view of the entire room and the rear of the dorm caught my attention first.

I noticed a group of inmates gathered around each other. At first glance I almost thought a fight was about to break out, but as I looked closer I recognized the circle and men knelt down to be a crap game. They were shooting craps for food items with the winner's pot scattered in a circle that consisted of packages of noodles, a variety of Little Debbie Snack Cakes, cans of tuna, packages of cookies, and of course cigarettes. On the other end of the room you had a group of inmates who occupied their time by doing pushups off the locker boxes, and curling buckets of rocks that had been gathered from the outside.

It also didn't take me long to notice that some of the most talented and creative people I had ever seen were behind bars. A person with the right mix of ingenuity and creativity could create almost anything in the dorm out of whatever they were given. From shower caddies with shoulder straps, to jewelry and chess pieces made from soap, if you wanted it inside you could have it, but it would cost you. To my rear I noticed another group of men that were gathered around one single inmate who entertained the crowd with a song.

I could tell that whatever the brother was talking about had to be interesting, cause he kept the attention of the group for at least an hour. The dayroom was more like the casino floor, because all day every day in each corner of the room nothing went on that didn't involve gambling. From poker, chess, dominos, and even war, everything was a hustle in prison, where everybody was trying to come up. It didn't take me long to realize that just about everything that goes on in the streets happens in prison, from gambling, to sex, and yes even drugs. Because I had no financial support from the outside, I had to rely on state pay, which gave inmates eighteen dollars a month that you could use on commissary.

Anybody that has ever been to prison will tell you that with eighteen dollars a month, it's really hard to make it despite factoring in three meals a day. So like most people who lack financial resources, I quickly fell into debt. The prison economy and its merchants relied and preyed on guys like me and they did so with "two for ones." Two for ones were agreements between the haves and the have-nots: you get one can of tuna, and when you get your state pay or go to the prison store your debt is two cans of tuna. One of the most lucrative hustles in prison was to operate a good store.

I knew a guy that made his living off of two for ones, and he had everything you needed from food to cigarettes, and even hygiene products. Running these stores were strictly prohibited in prison, and in order to run a successful one, you also had to have at least one other person that could hold merchandise for you in case of a random shakedown. During a shakedown, CO's could search your personal belongings and could tell if you were running a store, especially if you didn't have a good memory and you kept a list of people who owed you.

I had nothing but time on my hands and there was absolutely nothing to do while I was there. The very first day I got to prison CO's were removing all of the free weights and replacing them with universal weights. The thought behind the removal was lessening the potential for inmates to get bigger and stronger; but inmates still found a way despite their removal. I landed my first prison job in the chow hall serving food, but it was just a way to kill time because it didn't come with pay.

However, working in the chow hall had some major advantages for me, especially since I didn't have money to buy a whole lot of extra food from the commissary or stores. After everybody was served, I always had access to extra food, which was okay with me considering the serving portions were never enough. I was also able to sneak certain foods back to the dorm and sell them for other food items, or pay any outstanding debts.I made the most money when they served hamburgers, because I was able to get in good with the older cooks and get access to other condiments to help spice up what once was just a regular hamburger. I created my own personal Burger King sandwich every chance I could.

Every night all inmates were checked prior to leaving the chow hall, but most CO's didn't care about the food we took, they were more concerned about major contraband. There were nights especially in the wintertime when I would leave with so much food stored in pockets that it was a challenge to walk down the street. Since I didn't eat pork I'd also stand to barter and make a few deals on days where pork was on the menu. I would make my way to the back of the dorm and make a few deals for something that would hold me over till breakfast. My days working in the chow hall came to an end when I talked my way off the waiting list to obtain my GED.

Normally inmates that weren't facing much time didn't stand a chance of getting in, but I practically begged my way in. After I was done working in the kitchen I would show up across the street at the school and ask if I could help in the classrooms. While in the classrooms, I would help other inmates with basic reading and writing skills. The teachers and administrators took notice and asked me if I had my high school diploma. I showed up daily to the school helping others and when I wasn't helping others, I was helping myself by having conversations with teachers and building relationships with the administrators in hopes of them allowing me into the school program.

And to think that just a year prior, I was leaving school to go and make money to pay my bills and the thought of graduating late wasn't really important to me. Now I was incarcerated and the idea of being able to continue my education was exciting and I was willing to beg and show up every day in order to have the chance. I refused to be denied and I didn't know it at the time, but that was just the beginning of my academic pursuits.

Leaving the chow hall meant that I had to find new ways to survive and deal with my massive appetite. I started jumping the line throughout the day to make sure I got enough to eat. I'd stand in line, get my tray of food and sit down, then immediately get back in line for another tray. Sometimes line jumping worked because the CO on duty either wouldn't notice or wouldn't care. Other times it just resulted in being told to sit down and eat. We came up with some pretty clever schemes for line jumping.

The ones that worked best involved two or three other people. We would work together and distract those officers we knew had an issue with us eating multiple times. Once distracted, somebody would then jump in line. None of the other inmates ever told when this was being done. Other times we would just fall in line with the new group that was entering into the building, and not making contact with any of the officers so they wouldn't be able to tell that you were just in with a previous dorm. We'd also get creative with the food from the commissary.

The most popular dish was called "Breaks", which consisted of packages of Ramen noodles, crushed up Doritos Tortilla mayonnaise or other condiments, canned tuna, or any other form of canned meat that you could buy. The number of people who would contribute and eventually eat dictated the amount of food that was added. The noodles, which were the main ingredients and flavor, were all about personal preference. Mine happened to be chicken. The noodles were to be cooked by placing them in a bowl with hot water and placing a lid over it, and then mixed in with all of the other ingredients. After mixing and smashing, the ingredients would be spread out over a garbage bag like a big casserole.

The break was then covered with squeeze cheese, and barbeque sauce. To the outside world this may have sounded or looked gross, but in that environment it was the equivalent of a steak dinner. Sometimes inmates would chip in on a large break by bringing whatever they had that the other person didn't have to create one big meal. Inmates were able to get really fancy and creative with the meal by adding onions and green peppers that were usually taken from the chow hall. Eating a break was a sure way to put on the pounds and bulk up if you ate it all the time. Some inmates were able to get canned shrimp in their food boxes, and other luxury food from the outside, and would charge people to eat with them.

For some, you couldn't eat a break without drinking a foxy, which consisted of coffee and kool-aid and served over ice. This was a sure way to get inmates wired up, and this drink was considered the prison luxury drink because coffee was expensive. Because of the combination of caffeine and sugar, it was easy for many inmates to crave and develop slight addictions to foxies. There wasn't too much to be excited about in that place but the thought of starting my GED program was all consuming. The excitement made each day that drew me closer to it worth getting up and being productive.

My competitive nature caused me to be somewhat upset about not being in a position to graduate from high school simply because of the math portion of the Ohio Proficiency Test, but the school of hard knocks taught me not to cry more than a couple of tears over things like that. As a survival mechanism, I made it a habit to never walk into a room without sizing up everyone who was in there and locating all possible escape routes. If I was in a room full of predators, I'd be sure to sit with my back to a wall and never be surrounded or put my back to a door way. I had to be in a position to fight or take flight. To my surprise, the class of twenty or so inmates allowed me to take a break from being on edge. I was in a place where everyone was focused on learning and taking steps to make better of a second chance.

The instructor was very helpful in terms of working with us on a personal level with academic areas that we needed help in. Typically there was never any homework, but I always challenged myself and asked for math problems to take back to I-Dorm. There, I'd work on them while in the day room or in my bunk until I was sure they were correct. Sometimes just to have something to do I'd do them over and over again, even when I knew they were right. I'd turn them in the next day and wait for the grades. There were times in class when I grew bored but I didn't let my boredom be a distraction. I was able to remember what my distraction led to in Heritage middle school and I didn't want anything to get in the way of my success in the classroom.

My eagerness to get ahead and work with others was noticed, and soon I was allowed to stay after class while most rushed to leave at the end of the day. I also took time to help others on math problems in areas they were stuggling in. I received word one day from the teacher that they were allowing me to come into the GED program despite being nowhere near the top of the list to get into the program. The time I was spending in the classroom prior was just me taking the initiative I was able to take the practice tests that revealed my weakness in math but by the time the real test rolled around I was nervous as hell but I felt prepared.

The day of the test came with the most anxiety I'd felt in a long time but after praying before and after the test I realized that I had done all I could do. For once I wasn't worried about what the future had in store for me, and my anxiety was replaced with confidence. A few weeks had gone by when I received notice that I had indeed passed the test. The feeling of accomplishment was so overwhelming and was only rivaled by the feeling I felt when I was able to hold the actual paper in my hands.

I felt the burden of having not graduated from high school lift from my shoulders. Once I received notice, the first person that I called was my girlfriend, and I sent the diploma home to her for safe keeping. During my incarceration there were many things that could easily contribute to a bad day steeped in depression and sadness.

When this happened, it could be said that the time was doing the inmate, and not the inmate doing the time. Worrying about things that were out of my control led me down that path many, many times. My days always got the best of me when I decided to worry about what and who Tiffany was doing on the outside. There was a time period where I had not received a letter from her, and when I did it was very short. There had been a few weeks that passed from one letter to the next, so when one arrived I was extremely excited.

My excitement soon turned to a feeling of abandonment when her letter said that she couldn't continue to wait on me and was seeing another man. Reading that letter literally made me sick to my stomach, feeling even more upset because there was nothing I could do about it while I was there. It was a sense of powerlessness, emptiness, and complete lonesomeness. Having someone outside to lend moral support was a feeling that every man needed. Even if it were just looking forward to receiving mail or an occasional phone call, those little things meant so much, and to lose them in an instant was damaging.

I've seen men driven to tears and violence when the postman didn't have anything for them. Soon after receiving the break up letter, I received notice that I was to go before the parole board for shock parole. Inmates were eligible for shock parole once they had served at least six months of their sentence. The night before my hearing I prayed that God would help the parole board understand who I was and what had not happened in my case so that I could be released to a halfway house. If granted parole, I would have to wait at least 30 days for an open bed, and go to a halfway house on parole. I remember sitting in the hallway prior to going in with about six other inmates.

The waiting area was so quiet that I could hear my own heartbeat. I sat and meditated on trying to get my words right. For inmates who had much more time on their hands than I did, going to the parole board was a huge ordeal. Some who were sentenced to terms like five to twenty five years had no idea when they would be released due to indeterminate sentences.

As for me, even though I wanted early release, I knew I had an out date, and I also knew that no matter what they could only hold me for so long. I went into the room of two white males, and I think they could tell that I was nervous. They started the interview by asking me what happened the night of the crime. I politely explained to them that I had no idea as to what happened on that night; therefore, I couldn't explain to them what happened. They both looked at me as if they had heard that story before, and within three minutes it was all over. They handed me a piece of paper and told me to come back in six months when I felt remorseful for what I done.

One guy made the statement as I was leaving, "With the charges that were against you, you're lucky you got the time you got, at least you could say sorry."
As I took the walk back to the dorm, I reflected on the event that just took place. At first I was hurt that I had not been paroled, but when I thought about it more into the day, I realized that I had made the right decision. I figured that I had bowed down to the system once by pleading guilty in the first place, no way was I going to break down and make up some events that never took place.

My pride just would not allow me to do it, even if it was the difference between early release and serving my full sentence. It was always easy to spot others who had a bad day at parole board hearings. They would come in visibly upset; some mad, some crying, and go straight to their beds without saying a word to anyone. I once saw a guy come in after the parole board told him that they would reconsider his request in five more years. He fainted in the middle of the room and after being taking to the infirmary, he was then placed on suicide watch. Others would go into the parole board expecting bad news, knowing that it wasn't their time to go home.

There were even inmates who had become so accustomed to prison life that the thought of going home scared them. Some even committed offenses that would ensure that they stayed locked up. The thought that life as a free man was worse than living as a prisoner was a reality that I couldn't ever imagine being my own.

On rare occasions when the good news did come for inmates, a celebration usually followed. Individuals would have the free world equivalent to a cigar and cognac, which meant that we'd drink foxies and smoke Black and Mild cigars all night long. I didn't mind drinking, but never could get myself to smoke the cigars. Having so much down time in prison caused me to think and worry about my past and my future. I quickly learned that worrying about those two the way I was doing really affected my present. The time began to get to me and I grew tired of seeing the same people day in and day out.

Going through the same routine every minute of every day was enough to drive me insane. Depression and frustration set in and I knew it was only a matter of time before something happened that would make me act those feelings out. Around the time of my heaviest period of depression there started to be regular fights between inmates from different cities. It was mainly Columbus and Cleveland natives who chose to do battle.

The fights were mostly over bullshit but in prison most fights were. I tried my best not to get caught up in the mix but one particular day I had no choice. I was walking to the bathroom when I accidentally bumped into a guy from Cincinnati as we were both turning the corner. I said, "Excuse me, my fault man," and I wasn't expecting him to say sorry, but I also wasn't expecting his reaction. He stared me up and down and responded with, "Watch where you going you bitch ass nigga!"

Although I was interested in taking the high road, his response gave me a feeling in my gut that said it was about to be that moment I had been bottling up. Instead of a response that was more in line with his words I simply asked him why he had to say all that and explained that it was just an accident. He replied, "Cause it's like that you bitch ass Columbus nigga!" I noticed several other inmates from Columbus were listening and watching the whole ordeal. I knew that if I walked away I would be thrown to the wolves. Noone would respect me, and I would be a victim of future verbal and possibly physical assaults. I was done talking after that and done thinking too.

He began to look me up and down and before his eyes met mine again I had thrown a right hook that connected with his jaw. Once he fell to the floor I stood over him landing each right and left hook as close to his mouth as I could. With each blow I let out all of my anger and frustration, not against him, but against my current situation. His words sent me into an altered consciousness that I didn't snap out of until I was pulled from his bloodied face by a few COs.

I was on him so quickly and so viciously that he had no time to respond to the five or six blows to his face. My knuckles were swollen and bleeding from hitting his teeth, but that was the only evidence I wore from the fight. We both were handcuffed and rushed to solitary confinement or the hole as we came to know it. The hole is exactly what it sounds like: a very small cell with one bed, a small table, and a toilet. It was only big enough for me to walk either to the bed or to the door. The door had a slot that was used for passing meal trays through, and the meals were two-inch thick dry bologna and cheese sandwiches, a small low fat pint of milk, and a piece of fruit.

The cell stayed cold and the only company I had was the echo of whatever noise I made. Late nights in the hole were the hardest because it seemed like every inmate in the unit was up screaming and yelling at other inmates and demanding toilet paper and blankets from the officers. Those were the nights I spent trying to tire myself with sit-ups and pushups. It hardly ever worked and I would be forced to listen to the chaos until I happened to doze off. I spent a total of five days in the hole, which was a little longer than usual for the offense. When I finally did see the light of day, it was to go before the disciplinary committee. I entered the room where a five-person panel waited for me.

As I approached my chair the looks I received made me wonder if I had a foul odor or if the five white males just despised me. The violation was read aloud and one committee member asked me to explain what happened. Once I had given them my description of the events, I was found guilty. My punishment added three days to my sentence and took away my commissary for one month.

My release date was now pushed from the end of February to March 2, 1997. Three days may not sound like much, but for months I had a date locked into my mind and something to look forward to. Three minutes more would have been too much and three days now felt like an eternity was added. I was led back into regular population but the other guy was sent to a different dorm. Getting into that fight didn't help my chances once I returned to the parole board, but if it were anything like the first one, nothing would help me anyhow.

By the time I would see them again I had less than a year to go, and although it would have been nice to get out early, I went in with the same mindset I had the first time. Because I knew that I was standing on truth, I went in with a more confident and assertive attitude.

I knew regardless of what I said, I was going to have to do the rest of my time. I came in the room and sat quietly for a few minutes while they read over some of my paperwork. They watched for reactions as they read my charges aloud. The only expression I offered indicated that I was ready to leave and return to my dorm. After a few questions about how I was spending my time, he then asked me to explain what happened on that night.

In a very strong yet firm voice, I said to him, "Listen sir, I'll tell you like I told the last group of folks, like I told my public defender, like I told the victim, and the detective: I have no idea what happened on that night, because I wasn't there, and I can't explain something that I have no knowledge about." He paused for a second then replied, "So you don't feel remorseful about your actions?" I was done being respectful and went for the jugular. "Motherfucker, I don't feel remorseful about something I didn't do! Ask all them people involved in this shit, if they feel remorseful about locking my ass up, and ask that victim how he feels about picking the wrong person out of that line up!"

By this time I had stood up, and had my hand outstretched waiting on my papers. He suggested that I have a nice day as I snatched the papers out of his hand and was rushed out of the room and back to my dorm. The final months of my sentence mirrored my first few months; they were extremely hard to serve. It was like I had rolled, sat, and watched time pass a designated point only to find out that there was more that I didn't know about. I tried to engage in as many activities as I could to pass the time, and although I knew it wasn't, I found myself having a daily daydream where I played out my release day. It was at that point that the game of chess found me.

It was very common for inmates to learn to play and even more common for it to be a pastime of the more cerebral cons. I quickly learned that the game had a calming effect on me and it also allowed me to understand my decision making process and become more of a critical thinker. I had grown up knowing that often times I had to use what I had to get what I wanted. And for the times that I didn't have it, I had to figure out a way to get it. Once I began to play chess, I understood that it could be a model for how a man could live his life.

In order to survive and advance both in the game and in life, a man must be thoughtful about his actions and realize that each move has an outcome or reaction. In order to win, each move had to be more calculated than the previous one, and even when success wasn't guaranteed it was always most important to stay focused on the goal. As I learned more and my skills grew in the game, I began to compare everything around me to chess. I began to look at the reasons that most of us were incarcerated and I realized that in chess the game would be close to over for most if you lost your queen and the same was true of every man who had a voice that lead to his arrest and sentencing.

Pursuit of money, sex, and drugs were all ways of life for some folks, and not knowing how to survive without always meant that the game was just about over. I was also engaged in the flag football league, where I had established myself as one of the best running backs in the prison. I led my team to an undefeated season, and had a good reputation because of my skills. I remember the quarterback on my team telling me that I needed to be on somebody's football team once released from prison. I accepted and received his words and others who made that same comment on numerous occasions, including some officers, but I never actually thought I could after going to prison. Thirty days prior to release, I was placed in a pre-release program, which was supposed to prepare and support offenders as they readied for release.

Employment, housing, and life skills were supposed to be the areas of focus. The concept of the program was good, but the content turned out to be very poor. We were given handouts that at one point listed resources and job leads, but it only took a few minutes of reading to figure out that the information was outdated. The only thing I learned from that class was that having a good idea wasn't enough, there had to be some actual work put into making the idea work. The program didn't work for me; I didn't learn any info on jobs, nor did I know how to go about living the type of life that would allow me to leave the game alone and stay away from the criminal justice system.

It was anti-climactic because enrolling in the program was exciting. The program meant that I was one step closer to freedom, and it also meant that I got a special badge that let all the other inmates know that my days there were numbered. By the time I was down to my last thirty days, nothing time related mattered anymore. And even though those were the hardest days to serve, I always knew that each night and morning that followed brought me closer to getting out of that place. That last couple of weeks were really sobering and caused a bit of sadness. I was forced to deal with the fact that I had nowhere to go and more importantly, I had no plan of action.

I couldn't go back to the lifestyle I was living before I walked into the courthouse that day, but I also couldn't rely on a relative to allow me to stay until I got on my feet. All I owned was the clothes I was arrested in and things that I had once sent to my girlfriend. Before I could get down and depressed about my situation, I remembered the voice that I had heard in the beginning of my bondage. There was comfort in knowing that I had served all this time when I initially didn't think that I could. I was still alive, I hadn't been institutionalized, and I was wiser and stronger.

I was ready for the world but I didn't know quite what I was ready for. I would have never said it at the time, but I was scared. I had lost too much and learned too much to think that just because I wanted to be successful, that was going to be enough. My faith was reassured when a guy who was getting out about three days before me said that I could come and stay with him and his family until I was able to get on my feet. He and I had established a relationship over the past year, and I was so grateful.

I had also managed to make contact with the Columbus Urban League who offered a resource-based program that made contact with offenders who would be returning home to Columbus. After my initial contact the program manager, James King, wrote me back and provided some direction in terms of employment, and sent me enrollment brochures and flyers for Columbus State Community College. That was my plan: I would enroll in college once I got out. We exchanged letters a few times and in those letters I expressed my concern about the future.

He was very encouraging and provided concrete steps that I'd need to take in order to begin my new life. It was almost two years after my release when I bumped into him at a restaurant and he revealed to me that he was writing his first book. Mr. King shared that his book would be about his life on the down low (secretly having sexual relationships with men while engaging in sexual relationships with women) and that he had just signed a very lucrative book deal. Our interactions were always professional and although I was in shock, I respected that he had enough courage to write a book that revealed so much of his personal life.

I never would have guessed that he was secretly living the type of lifestyle that he shared his book was about. During the last two days of my prison sentence, I took the time to say goodbye to folks that I had learned from and that I was grateful to have shared my experience with. People on the outside of prison walls have no idea what talent, ingenuity and creativity exist in where seemingly it would be dark and devoid of any redeeming qualities.

The last Saturday night while most inmates were up late, I lay on my bed and reflected on the past two years. All I could think about was how angry I was, how much I resented the system, how sad I had been, and yet I was still hopeful. I looked around the room and wondered how many of these men I'd see again and I also took mental note of all the things I wouldn't miss. Although the days were long, and I had many sleepless nights, I did have something to be proud of: I had obtained my GED, and I had every intention of enrolling in college and earning a degree. I had already received information from Columbus State Community College on steps to enroll.

I was excited about being released yet very nervous about what was waiting for me on the outside. I had taken the time to think about some of the things that I wanted to do, but still lacked the confidence and insight on how to begin my new journey. In a way, I was changed. I was wiser. I was more of a critical thinker, and I was sure that a life of crime was not for me. Then the harshest of realities hit me when I realized that no one was excited that I was coming home and I was leaving the same way I had come in-- alone. However, I was anxious about returning home to see Tiffany despite knowing that she had been with other brothers while I was down.

I was uncertain about what the future had in store for us after she hurt me during my time in. She never visited or sent me money, but she was all I had. That Sunday morning, March 2, 1997, after spending 488 days in three different correctional institutions, I was finally a free man. Excitement woke me up at 5:00 am, long before the dorm lights even came on. I sat eagerly on my bunk waiting for my last name and number to be called. The little belongings that I did have were already packed up, and the things that I didn't want or couldn't take with me, other inmates had already laid claim to.

Nervous energy kicked in and at one point I lost track of time and dozed off until I heard the dorm intercom system. "Wilson, 325-675, pack it up and roll it out!" Those words were like music to my ears and to date, one of the best feelings ever. As I carried my box back up the hill I could still remember the first day and heading the opposite direction with the opposite emotions. The walk seemed to take forever, like it was all of a sudden much longer.

Many approached me and said their goodbyes and words of encouragement. After filling out some paperwork and getting my release papers, I was escorted along with others who were being released through the visiting lobby and to the gates. As I walked through the gates towards a waiting van, I turned back and watched them close slowly. It felt good to finally be on this side of the cage. The air smelled sweeter, the ground felt a little softer, and because of all that was behind me and ahead of me, I vowed to never return.

"The secret of change is to focus all of your energy, not on fighting the old, but on building the new"
~Socrates

COMING HOME

I was more afraid leaving prison than I was two years prior when I first arrived. Arriving on that day and receiving instructions about where to walk, what to expect, and the routine I would follow was easy because there was always someone telling me what to do and how to conduct myself. The outside world would involve none of that and not only did it require me to fend for myself, it also presented me with situations that could lead me back to the place I swore to never return. I had more questions but mentally devoid of any solid plans that would help me reach my goals.

A major contributing factor to my anxiety was knowing that I didn't know how to conduct myself socially based on what I knew I needed to do and who I needed to become. The small gray minivan that drove me through the hills on route 33 towards Columbus seemed to move slowly enough for me to revisit my past. As the wheels turned, so did the chapters in my mind. I saw myself playing football in Lincoln Park Projects, in science class in Heritage Middle School, on the football field at Independence High School, in my apartment, and finally in a shootout in a small town over drugs.

The flashbacks stopped when I was dropped off at the Greyhound bus station, handed seventy-five dollars, and sent on my way. There I stood, dressed in my prison blues and rust-colored boots taking it all in. I was finally free. A smell that I dreamt about while laying on my bunk filled my lungs. I followed my nose and it led me past a few "Welcome Home" greetings from bus station workers, and straight to Burger King. It was obvious that the bus station employees had become fans of seeing people in prison blues and knew we had just been dropped off. I responded to their greeting, "Thank you, it feels good to be home."

Burger King was the candy store, and I was a fat kid who was about to indulge. The cashier was a friendly young lady who smiled and greeted me by also saying, "Welcome home." I responded with a quick, "Thanks. So yeah umm, let me get a double whopper with cheese combo, with a large drink." I carried my tray to the condiment section, grabbed some napkins, salt, and ketchup then sat down by myself. I began to inhale the food with such speed that I hardly tasted it. As I sat with my elbows on the table surrounding my tray, one of the guys cleaning tables noticed how fast I was eating and said, "Say youngblood, you not down no more man. Slow down, ain't no time frame. Nobody gon' take it from you if you not done in 5-7 minutes."

I paused for a second to take in his words that made perfect sense, and I made sure that the last couple of bites were taken with every intention of enjoying the moment. The mess I made on my shirt made it very clear that the food was good and that moment was one I thought about for months. I found a payphone and the first call I made was to my brother whom I had not talked to in months. He still resided with my great- aunt and had no idea that I was coming home. After two rings, my great-aunt picked up the phone and once she noticed it was me, she shared her excitement because she knew just how happy Jamil would be to see me. When my ten-year-old brother was given the phone and said hello, his voice made the tears begin to flow.

I was so chocked up that I could hardly respond to his words. I managed to get out a, "Hey J," in a low voice while trying to disguise the fact that I was now crying. His excitement to hear my voice made the tears come down even more. His first words to me were, "Rayshawn, when you coming home?" I paused for a few seconds before I informed him that I was home. He screamed loud for everyone in the house, "My brother is out!" Going to see him was my first priority. Hearing the joy in his voice warmed my heart and I let him know that I would be coming to see him on the following day. My next phone call was to my ex-girlfriend. She knew that I was coming home, but had made it clear that she didn't want to see me until she was done with her final exams.

My sudden incarceration left her feeling empty and abandoned in many ways, but she was still excited that I was home. Although I was hurt by her words and actions while I was locked down and our future was uncertain, I couldn't deny that I still loved her. After a few calls were made at the payphone, reality set in. I realized that I had no real place to go and call home. While I was locked up, I became really close to a guy named Moss who was released a few days prior. He gave me his number and told me that if I needed a place to stay to contact him.

Although I had developed a good relationship with him, people in prison tell lies and use situations like that to establish loyalty, so I didn't believe him. I did manage to keep in touch with a girl I knew before going to prison. She also mentioned that I could stay with her a few days until I figured out what my next move was going to be. Those few days ended after just one day. Almost immediately upon entering her apartment we began having sex. Having sex after two years was explosive and much like that Whopper combo meal, nothing compared to the feeling of wanting and visualizing something for so long then finally getting it. It was like I had my first sexual experience all over again.

That night she made it known that she wanted to be in a relationship with me and instantly I was uncomfortable. It placed me in a difficult situation, on one hand I needed a place to stay and I knew she could provide that for me. On the other hand, the commitment was something that I knew I didn't want. Out of my desire for self-preservation and out of not wanting to hurt her feelings, I held her tight and said I wanted nothing more than to be with her. Early the next morning I woke up before she did and while she was still sleeping I eased out of bed and put on my clothes. I quietly walked down the stairs to leave.

Prior to walking out of her apartment I noticed her purse sitting nearby. I approached it, looked inside, and noticed three crisp twenty-dollar bills. I pocketed them and walked out of her apartment never to be seen by her again. I had learned to seize the moment and to take advantage of opportunities that were in front of me. I also knew that staying with a girl who wanted to be with me would lead to drama and I didn't want any more drama. After satisfying my top two cravings, my next mission was to be free of the clothes that were a reminder of prison life to me and anyone else who saw me.

I rode the transit bus to the Far East Side where I used to live. There I found a thrift store that I was familiar with. It didn't take me long to find a couple pairs of decent used jeans, shirts, and one pair of old Nike sneakers that were still in good shape. Once I paid for the items I immediately went to the dressing room to put on the new clothes. I donated the prison clothes and left them there. For twenty dollars I had just become respectable. Leaving those clothes there felt as if I were leaving the past exactly where it needed to be, with the rest of the stuff that nobody wanted.

It wasn't long before school was out and as promised, I made my way to see my brother. The moment we embraced the tears began to flow again. It had been well over two years since I had seen him. Prior to my conviction even though we were in the same city, being bounced around different foster homes and group homes led to our contact being minimal. At this point he was living with our great-aunt and two older cousins. The conditions of the neighborhood he lived in were by far some of the worst conditions I had ever seen and to make matters worse, our two older cousins were involved with drugs. As I sat there with my brother, I watched the traffic coming in and out with my cousins hardly even noticing that I was there.

Due to health and old age, my aunt didn't say or do much other than sit and watch television. She had a history of raising kids in the family and for that she was loved, but not respected by my two cousins based on how they treated the conditions of her house. I learned that my own mother spent much of her time with Aunt Alma, along with another one of my great-aunts. Aunt Alma also raised those two cousins after their mom, for unknown reasons, wanted nothing to do with them. She was the only one in the family who was willing to take my brother in. She even offered for me to stay with her, my cousins, and my brother but I just couldn't do it.

My brother had spent so much time with my Aunt Alma from such an early age that he was used to being around her. As I engaged in conversation with my brother trying to catch up on things, I couldn't help but look out the living room window and notice crack being sold right outside. My attention was then immediately drawn to a tiny mouse running along the baseboard of the living room. Jamil, although young, was very smart and just shook his head, "Man this is what I deal with every single day around here." My heart dropped as I became sad for him and wanted to do something that could eliminate the need for him to live in those conditions.

For as much as I wanted to do something, I realized there was nothing I could do except get myself together so that I could help him in the future. I turned my attention to my own survival when Jamil asked me where I was living. I had no words for him because I didn't know or have a clue where I was going to call home. Although I couldn't provide him with where I was going, I did promise him that I would never go back to prison again and I would always do my best to be there for him. The look in his eyes told me that he didn't want to see me go, and as I hugged him and got ready to make my way out the door, I noticed one of my cousins walking out from one of the bedrooms. With the windows open, the air blew in the smell of crack cocaine and it traveled right through the living room. We both were headed towards the front door and before he opened the front door I stopped him. "Man, why ya'll got this shit all up in this house and in front of my brother? He's too young to be around all of this."

He quickly replied, "Rayshawn, you ain't been around in years doing shit for Jamil, so don't come running up in here like you better than anybody trying to tell people what to do. While your ass was running around selling the shit, everybody else up in this house has been taking care of your brother. Where were you then? Cause you damn sure ain't put no money up in here to provide for him." His words cut like a box cutter and they hurt, not because what I said to him was wrong, but because what he said was the truth. He continued his stride to a car that awaited him at the curb.

Before I left the house, I reached in my pocket and pulled out my friend Moss's phone number. It was time to see if he would hold true to his word and provide me with a place to stay until I figured things out. When he answered the phone I let out a sigh of relief that it was the correct number. He provided me with his address and told me to come see him. He lived on the corner of Livingston Avenue and Oakwood, an area that I was familiar with. As a child, this was the first street we lived on when we moved from California to Ohio. The neighborhood had taken a turn for the worse since crack cocaine and gangs were having their way all up and down the blocks of the East Side.

The corner played out a familiar scene of dope boys hanging on the corner waiting to make a sale. As I walked by, I remembered my time as a corner boy and longed for the money I knew filled their pockets, but I also knew that the money wasn't worth my freedom. The allure of the game was enticing but just as quick as it had crossed my mind, the thoughts of those prison gates popped in my head. The thought of going back to prison scared the shit out of me. As I approached his two-story house, Moss came running out of the door to greet me with open arms.

He hugged me tightly and offered me to come inside. Once inside he introduced me to his beautiful wife and five kids, who were all under the age of thirteen. "Man I've been expecting you and wondered if you were okay, or if you would call at all. I've already told my wife about you so if you still need a place to stay you're more than welcome." I stood there in his living room speechless. It was almost as if I was living a dream and this man would allow me to stay in his house with his wife and five kids. Moss and I spent countless hours with each other while in prison, and we looked out for each other as much as we could. This was not the first time Moss had looked out for me.

There were times when I was on the verge of hunger and Moss would provide for me with no questions. We hung out a lot on the prison yard together, and when I was able to return the favor with food, I would. But he never expected anything and from him I began to learn lessons in loyalty. This situation was no different.

I asked him how much he wanted me to pay him and he replied, "Man listen, I want you to first focus on getting yourself a job. My kids and my family are okay and whatever you are able to give, I'm positive that you'll do that." He moved one of his kids out of a room and into another room to allow me to have my own space. I promised him that in just a few weeks I would get a job and make sure that I gave something on regular basis and assured him that I wouldn't need long to get on my feet. Once I was in the bedroom, I laid down on my back. I looked up towards the ceiling and I was immediately reminded of God's voice my first night in prison and the words that He spoke to me. He told me that no matter what happens from this day forward, He would protect me.

Being reminded of those words, I was soon filled with so much emotion that I started to cry uncontrollably. I looked past the ceiling to the sky and with all of the emotion that spilled from my eyes and mouth I simply said, "Thank you Lord! Thank you." Two weeks later after filling out countless job applications and being rejected at every turn, my breakthrough came. I landed a third shift job at the City Center Mall working as a janitor. I was responsible for cleaning glass, running the vacuum throughout the carpeted areas of the mall, buffing floors, and emptying garbage cans. My supervisor had been there for some years and he too had spent time in prison, so he had no problem or reservations about hiring me.

I remember when he was looking over my application during my interview and he got to the part where I had to mark down that I was a convicted felon; he stopped and just looked at me. Scared that I was again about to be rejected for yet another job due to the felony, before he could even say anything I told him, "Listen man, I'm a hard worker and hands down I'm the best person for this job. All I'm asking for is an opportunity and a chance." He smiled and damn near laughed at me. Confused and slightly disappointed, I was getting ready to get up and walk out. Before I stood to get out of my seat, he praised me and shared that he had never seen anyone interview the way I did for a job. He told me that if the way I interviewed was any indication of how I would be as an employee, I was hired. Just as promised, I worked my butt off on that job. There were times when I worked a double shift to make some extra money. During those times, I cleaned the filthy public restrooms and scrubbed up messes that literally made my stomach turn.

No matter how messy or how degrading it was to clean up after people, it felt good to have an honest and legal job that would allow me to earn money and stay out of trouble. The sense of pride that came from a hard day's work was a feeling that made me realize that I had been missing that feeling all along. Excited about my first paycheck due to all the hours I had worked, I was disappointed when I opened the check up to see that it was only for five hundred dollars. Uncle Sam with his taxes took almost as much as I got to bring home. It was not the kind of money I was accustomed to making, but I took that money and made it work.

The first thing I did was give Moss and his wife $150. I provided some food for myself, bought two inexpensive outfits, saved money for me to ride the bus back and forth to work, and put the rest in the bank of Rayshawn Wilson, which was located under the mattress. I busted my butt on that job for well over six months. I did a good job saving money, was able to open up a real savings account, and continued to make sure that I was providing money to Moss. During that time I found it hard for me to sleep many nights. I would often wake up in the middle of the night from nightmares.

One particular night I suddenly woke up thinking I heard a correctional officer yelling for me to state my inmate number. I jumped out of the bed yelling, "325-675 Wilson sir!" I awakened to find myself soaked in sweat and confused by the sounds of police sirens nearby. The confusion soon passed and I was reminded that I was no longer locked up. There would be many of those dreams after the first one, even months after being released from prison. After staying with Moss and his family for about eight months, I left the comfort of his home and family when I was able to get my own apartment. It was a real struggle finding anyone who would rent to me due to my felony conviction.

I was being turned away even in the bad areas of Columbus. I ran into a guy that I had known in my childhood who had some property that had an upstairs apartment that he was willing to rent to me. Because of our relationship, he rented to me for a reduced rate. By this time, I had landed a job at OSU hospital as a Patient Service Associate. I was responsible for cleaning patient's rooms and pushing them to different testing sites.

Once again I interviewed well for the position by selling my ambition and my ability to be a team player. Having only been out of prison for less than a year, things were going in the right direction. I was beginning to feel a sense of accomplishment. My ex-girlfriend and I were hanging out at my apartment one particular evening and after falling asleep, I was awakened by a tap on my shoulder. She whispered that she heard someone in the kitchen. I rose up slowly and fixed my ear to the air so I could hear what was going on in the kitchen. It sounded as if whoever was in the kitchen was going through a grocery bag. I slowly got out of the bed and started to walk towards the kitchen.

I remember being scared but I grew more upset with each step that brought me closer to the kitchen. The closer I got the louder the sound became. Once I reached the kitchen, I immediately turned on the light expecting to see someone standing in the kitchen robbing me of my food. Instead, I found a grey alley rat the size of my foot. The rat had eaten his way through a package of Ramen Noodles and decided to stay in the kitchen and finish the meal. Upon turning the light on the rat shot across the kitchen floor and hid behind the stove. I ran back towards the bed and told my girl what it was.

Of course the likely reaction was a scream, but she also grabbed her clothes and let me know that she could not stay. I picked up the phone to call the landlord and notify him without even considering the late hour. It was after 1:00am on a work night, and he was not happy that I had called him. To make matters worse, we had already exchanged words recently when I demanded that he fix up the place to make it more livable.

Apparently, I wasn't grateful enough for him and he was not too happy with me calling him in the wee hours of the night waking him and his family. He told me I had thirty days to vacate his property and he hung up the phone. By this time my girl had gone home, and there I was left with that damn rat. It all seemed like it was too good to be true, but I was determined to continue with my progress. Neither a rat, nor a slumlord could stop me from doing what I was learning was a part of my newfound hustle, working hard and enjoying the fruits of my labor.

I did everything I could to find a place to stay within that thirty- day timeframe. No place would rent to me and it was a huge waiting list to get into any boarding rooms, or even down at the YMCA. With about two days before I was due to leave, my luck went further south. While at work, I was caught sleeping on the job in the lobby area of my floor. They had been paging me several times to come clean a patient's room and I thought I had my pager set to vibrate, but it was silenced.

I was still on my ninety-day probationary period, and I was fired on the spot. No job, lost the benefits, no place to stay, and I had no one to turn to. As I packed up my clothes, a phone number fell from one of my pants pocket. It was a number from this girl, Ms. Perry, that I had met at the bus stop one morning on my way to work. I had only spoken to her a few times since we first met. I called her and after some brief conversation I asked if I could come over. After a few visits and a few sexual encounters, I started to make my way over to her apartment more frequently.

When I wasn't with her, I was sneaking in and out of my girlfriend's dorm room in Canfield Hall at Ohio State University. They were not allowed to have boys in the room after a certain hour, so the days I would be there I knew I had to come in early and remain quiet. Those nights were especially rough because I had to sneak around for everything and risked her getting in trouble and being kicked out. I didn't have access to the restroom so when nature called I used glass bottles. She would get in good with the RA's at times and they would turn a blind eye to me sneaking to the male wing of the building for showers.

She hadn't been there for me when I was locked up, but she stepped up and helped me in one of the most crucial periods of my life. It turned out that's when I needed her the most. She helped me survive and she knew nothing of the other girl I was staying with on nights when I wasn't with her. She thought I was staying at a relative's house. It was a dirty game that I played for months but to me it was survival.

It was always hard keeping them away from each other, but I did so with great creativity because my livelihood depended on it. Within a short period of time, my plan worked out as I wanted it to with Ms. Perry allowing me to stay with her full-time. Because her feelings started to grow quickly for me, she soon began to ask questions about where I was going overnight. I told her that I was caring for my great-aunt on those nights because those were the nights nobody was there to care for her.

When my girlfriend picked me up, I told Ms. Perry she was my cousin taking me to our aunt's house. My girlfriend never questioned much, and when she came to pick me up she didn't even need to get out of the car because I was typically there to meet her. Not only was it a struggle to maintain the lies, but it was also a struggle juggling my time, our sex lives, and the emotional aspects of a relationship. Add that to the fact that I was able to land a job at the Boys & Girls Club and I started going to Columbus State Community College, I felt as if I had four full-time jobs. The struggle was real but it I had a nice routine going. I was settled with my job working with kids at the Boys & Girls Club, school was going well, and I had no issues.

Many men who juggle more than one woman know they are bound to slip up and it was only a matter of time before I did. One hot summer day I was at a local pool not too far from where Ms. Perry lived. I remember being with a couple of male friends just hanging out when my pager started blowing up with both numbers from Ms. Perry and my girlfriend's dorm room. I knew nothing good was coming from this, and I jumped into my car and headed to Ms. Perry. Once I was parked in front of her apartment, I noticed she was throwing all of my clothes out of the window.

It drew a crowd from the neighbors and as I jumped out the car I ran up the steps to one angry and hurt woman. Somehow my girlfriend got Ms. Perry's number and called to ask for me. Ms. Perry thought it was my cousin because we both shared the same last name. My girlfriend politely informed Ms. Perry that she was my girlfriend, and the shit hit the fan from there. Although I tried to explain, the damage was done and I was asked to leave. I gathered my belongings and packed everything I owned into the trunk of my car. I had no idea what I was going to do or where I was going to go. But my survival skills wouldn't let me fail. I might have been down, but I was on my way back up.

"Education is the most powerful weapon you can use to change the world"
~Nelson Mandela

COLLEGE DAYS SWIFTLY PASS

Inmates spend so much time in the prison system talking about what they will do when they are finally free. Some talk about the first good meal they'll consume, others about spending time with loved ones and lovers, some even talk about kissing the ground of the free world. The rare occasion when I found myself verbalizing my intentions to go to college and even play college football, I was all but laughed at and my words were immediately dismissed by some while encouraged by others who witnessed what I could do on the field in the flag football league. They reacted as if I had talked about flying to the moon on a magic carpet.

To the men around me it was a fantasy, but to me it was the ambition that would fuel my journey once I was free. My first act of ambitious defiance was writing to Columbus State Community College to request information about the college, majors, and programs of study. I remember the looks of curiosity that came my way when that big envelope came since inmates generally did not get large envelopes unless they contained legal documents from an attorney. I tucked the package away and waited until it was quiet in the dorm room when most inmates were asleep to review the information.

Sometimes the background noise in that place was deafening and I wanted to explore my future in peace and quiet. I didn't know what I wanted to do or what I wanted to study, but I knew college was the only option that felt like it would lead me where I wanted to go. Three months after my release, I completed placement exams and the financial aid applications. Soon I was accepted and enrolled in Columbus State Community College. My next challenge was determining which classes to take. I knew more about how to survive and navigate the world I was leaving than I did about the one I was entering.

It scared me just as much as my first night of incarceration. I spent at least three hours in the school's library trying to figure everything out. Finally, something sounded appealing to me: Introduction to Sociology. Studying people and their actions in the world was something I always did out of my need to survive, and the thought of getting an education and eventually making a career out of it made sociology seem like it was designed with me in mind. I then added some of the courses I knew I needed in order to be successful, like English and Math. Stepping into that class on the first day brought back memories of elementary school when I would be so excited the night before the first day of school.

The only difference was I wasn't worried about a new outfit, what I had for lunch, or which friends would be there. I was on a solo mission, and nothing outside of realizing my dreams and reaching my goals mattered. The sociology class proved to be very exciting and I looked forward to it even on days when class was not scheduled. Studying people, discussing social groups, structures, processes, institutions, and events was indeed what I was supposed to be doing. To dig deeper into subject matters dealing with social structure, deviance, social inequality, race and gender were all topics that sparked my interest and I couldn't wait to further my education.

Having never received good grades in high school, I was pleased that studying at the college level came quite easily for me in most social science classes. My first quarter was beyond successful. I earned an A in Sociology, an A in English, and a B in Math. When I received the print out, I had to double check the name to make sure it was mine at the top of the grade report. In all of my years of school, I couldn't remember a time where I had good grades, not even in physical education. My immediate success made me feel so good about myself and accomplishing my goals that I was excited to start the next quarter. Most of all, I had proven to myself that I was not just a dreamer, I was a doer. Before the start of the next quarter I was walking through a building and came across a table set up with a banner behind it that said Otterbein College.

Two representatives were standing behind the table, one a student and one a staff member. I walked slowly past the table and just when I was getting ready to pass it up, an older black woman stopped me. "Say young man, what do you know about Otterbein College," she asked. I approached the table acknowledging that I knew nothing about the school except that it was located up in Westerville. She provided me with some information about the school including a list of majors, her card, and asked that I give her a call soon. I thanked Mrs. Gene Talley and the student (who would introduce herself as Chinyere Amaefule) and shoved the materials into my book bag as I walked away.

It would be a few days later after that exchange while sitting in the cafeteria when I would pull out all of the information they provided and begin to look through it. While I knew I had every desire to transfer to a four-year college, I had no idea where I wanted to go or if I could even get in to any school. After looking through the academic part I came across information about their football program which immediately grabbed my interest. Not soon after going over the materials I went and called Mrs. Talley, who was the Associate Director of Admissions responsible for recruiting students of color to Otterbein. While on the phone I gave her as much of my background as I could for an introduction. I included my high school grades, which were below a 2.0 GPA, my ACT/SAT scores, and my current grades at Columbus State.

My ACT score was an eleven, which would indicate to most that I had about a sixth-grade education before earning my GED, but I didn't feel ashamed because I was able to show where I was now as a student. Mrs. Talley gave me hope that I could still get into Otterbein College provided that I had strong grades the rest of the year at Columbus State. She also advised me as to which classes to take in order to ensure they would transfer over and help my case. She didn't promise me anything, but told me if I did my part in school she would do everything that she could to fight for my acceptance into Otterbein in the fall of 1998. I left that conversation excited and nervous about the challenge of the grades I had to obtain in order to even be considered.

Although I had put up some pretty decent grades thus far, the classes she wanted me to take (including college level math) were intimidating. I accepted the challenge and the next quarter I dropped classes I had chosen and picked up classes that she suggested. The quarter would be as challenging as I expected and it was mainly because of the math course. During week three, I was already failing the class but it wasn't due to a lack of effort. As an added burden, I was also homeless during this time. I went back and forth between Tiffany's dorm room at OSU, and sleeping in my car at Franklin Park.

I made friends with a classmate and I would go to his house to study at night and manage to conveniently fall asleep until morning. I was working part time, third shift at a warehouse packing sales flyers into large bags that would be distributed in the mail. I hated that job with a passion, but it was my only source of income and quite frankly, I had to earn to learn. Some weeks I was working forty or more hours on third shift. I would get off of work, sleep for a few hours, and make it to campus where I was taking a full course load. This process went on for so long it was as if I were on autopilot. I also did not have access to a computer off campus so I had to spend a lot of time in school library gathering as much information as I could between classes and right before having to be at work.

The rigor of my schedule started to take a toll on me and it was noticeable in some of my coursework. I would check in with Mrs. Talley often, informing her that everything was fine knowing that it was only the partial truth. Since math was the class that was causing me the most problems, I made it my business to speak to my professor regularly to seek additional help when I was struggling. I refused to fail without fighting. I would often show up to his office prior to class and I'd even stop him in the halls just to make sure I was getting the help I needed. Because he saw the energy I was putting into being successful, not only did he help me but he also allowed additional time during tests. Not having to rush when it came to figuring out how to order my steps and complete the problems made all the difference.

Midway into the quarter I received a letter from the head coach at Otterbein requesting that I contact them to set up a campus visit. Getting that letter brought a smile to my face as I pictured myself playing the game that I always loved. My high school glory was short-lived and because of so many factors I also felt like the dream was never realized. This letter breathed life back into that dream. The hard work during those ten weeks paid off as I managed to get a B- in the math class, and two A's in my other classes, ending the quarter with well over a 3.0 GPA. I had earned a 3.5 GPA for the year. I then submitted my application and additional materials to Otterbein College for consideration. While waiting on the decision from Otterbein's admission office, my attention and energy was focused on surviving.

It was the summer time now and Tiffany was home living with her mother, so the occasional dorm living was out of the question. Her mother still didn't care much for me, so I would only go to her house when she wasn't home. During the day, after third shift ended, I'd go by to take a shower, sleep for a little and have a meal. I had no excuse to stay at my classmate's house anymore since school was out of session, so during the nights I didn't have to work I was able to stay at The Friends of Homeless Shelter on East Main Street. I knew one of the nightshift workers there, and he would sometimes risk his job to let me in late at night when most people were asleep. Many nights, by the time I got there, the beds were full so I would have to make due and find space wherever I could.

The conditions in that place were unimaginable. The smell hit me like a ton of bricks the moment I walked in the door and the smell was just as bad as the appearance. It was centered in a neighborhood that was saturated with crime and drugs. Regardless of the smell and feel of the place, I was always thankful to have a place to lay my head and not have to worry about being a victim. I would get up early enough to wash up and leave before anyone would realize that I wasn't supposed to be there. Not only did I not meet the criteria to be called homeless, I also couldn't meet the curfew demands that were placed on residents.

After the long wait, on a day in mid-July while I was at Tiffany's house, my cell phone rang and I noticed the "823" prefix which was an indication that the call was coming from Otterbein. I handled the phone like it was on fire while trying to answer it. Once I was able to hold it to my ear and say hello I heard Mrs. Talley's voice. I stood in the middle of the living room during the phone call, and the small talk we typically engaged in only made my anxiety level higher. When my anxiety was at its highest, she shared that the admissions committee had met and reviewed my file, and that I had been accepted into Otterbein College. After hearing those words I dropped the phone, fell to my knees, and began crying tears of joy.

This was such a new feeling. Prior to that moment, my tears had only come from sorrow and pain. However, at that moment, I was filled with so much emotion that I forgot Mrs. Talley was on the phone. Tiffany picked the phone up for me and finished the conversation. I was instructed to report to the financial aid office to go over my financial aid package, and also schedule a time to meet with the football coaches. After I gathered myself together and started to reflect on the news, I realized that the day was also the same date in July that I was accused of robbing and stabbing that guy. I was just over one year removed from being released from a state prison, and soon I would be entering a different type of institution, an institution of higher learning at Otterbein College.

I was up bright and early the next day to head to the school as instructed. My excitement and enthusiasm was obvious in that I was there ten minutes before the doors of the financial aid office even opened. I eagerly introduced myself and the lady who was about to help me already had my file on her desk. We went over my financial aid package which indicated that I would receive a substantial amount of money due to me being a ward of the court. Having neither of my parents around meant that I would be classified as an independent student. She went over the paperwork that declared that I would not have to pay any out of pocket expenses except whatever was necessary to buy my books.

With the amount of money I was to receive, I would actually be getting money back that I could use for living expenses. After signing all of the necessary papers, I headed to the football offices. I walked past the football field where I observed several players working out and going through a series of drills. I watched for a few more minutes before making my way into the building where I would meet the coach that I had been in contact with. As he greeted and welcomed me into his office, he invited me to have a seat. He then stated that he would be right back and needed to get a packet for me.

I looked on the board and noticed the offensive depth chart and beside the chart was a list that named notable incoming freshman/ transfer students. It was a wonderful feeling to see my name on the board even though I was noted fourth on the depth chart. Just to be up there was a wonderful feeling. After a few short minutes he returned handing me a packet of information that included a workout schedule and when to report to camp. He informed me that on the first day of camp I would be tested in the areas listed. Bench press, vertical jump, forty-yard dash, shuttle run, and the list went on and all that became clear was that I had work to do. He told me that although I had not played a down of football in over three years, he was sure that I could adjust and learn the offense and find my way on the field in no time. Based on Mrs. Talley's suggestion, my final stop for the day was the Student Affairs Office to speak with a man named Darryl Peal.

As I entered into the small building, I was greeted by the receptionist who then directed me to his office. The door was open and I knocked. Although he was talking to another staff member, he greeted me to come in without even looking up. "Can I help you," he asked. I replied, "I'm a new student for this fall and Mrs. Talley suggested that I come talk to you, but I'm not sure why." He asked if my parents were with me and I shared that my mom was in prison and my dad was dead. He then paused and stood looking at me like I had said something in a foreign language, as did his co-worker, who would later introduce himself to me as Bo Chilton, Director of Career Services.

Mr. Peal thought I was a traditional freshman at 18-years-old and asked me what high school from which I had recently graduated. Growing somewhat tired with the questions I stated, "Listen man I'm 20-years-old, a transfer student from Columbus State, I just did two years in prison for a crime I didn't commit, I don't know anything about college except that I'm here majoring in sociology and I'll be playing football this fall." They both kind of looked at each other, asked me to shut the door and have a seat. Bo also took a seat not too far away from me. He asked me some additional questions about my life and asked if anyone else knew about my background.

I informed him that no one knew except Mrs. Talley, and even she didn't know everything or what I had been through to get here. He paused for a brief second looked at Bo then told me, "Here's what I'm going to do. First off, you are not going to be staying in the dorms. I'm going to place you in one of our theme houses with three other black men, who are going to make sure that you are okay and that you are going to graduate from this school. Don't mention to many people that you have been to prison just yet, except for your roommates. These men are members of my fraternity who are about their business and also on pace to graduate."

Having very little knowledge about Black Greek fraternities, I asked if they were members of Kappa Alpha Psi. They both looked at each other and laughed, while indicating that they were members of Alpha Phi Alpha Fraternity, Inc., the first black Greek organization to be established. He then proclaimed that one day I too would be an Alpha man. At the time that was not important to me, I simply wanted to know where I was living, and how to get the meal plan that guaranteed me three meals a day. I was on the verge of not having to worry about a roof over my head or food in my belly, and I could feel conversation between the three of us lasted for well over an hour, and they both provided me with their phone numbers and told me to be in touch and visit with them regularly. Over a month after that conversation I found myself sitting in the auditorium for new student orientation weekend.

The auditorium was soon packed with students and as I looked around the room, it was very obvious that there were not too many students here that looked like me. Otterbein had a predominately white student population settled in a predominately white city in Westerville, Ohio, and in the back of my mind I wondered where I would fit in there. Founded in 1847 before the abolition of slavery, the campus was birthed by a rich tradition of people both white and black that worked to ensure social justice through women's suffrage, the abolitionist movement, and the Underground Railroad.

Historically, Otterbein is known as one of the first colleges in the United States to admit women, and I quickly learned that the same spirit that spearheaded those movements was still alive and well on that campus. Two weeks after new student orientation, I was set to report to football camp. The night before training camp I had a hard time sleeping because I was full of excitement and anxiety. I didn't know what to expect but whatever it was, I sure was ready for it. I lay there in bed visualizing running the ball, scoring touchdowns, and college football fame. I could hear the sports announcer over the loud speaker calling my name each time I carried the ball. "First down. Rayshawn Wilson on the carry!"

On the morning of camp check-in, I arrived at the dorms and cars were lined up everywhere as football players moved their televisions, gaming systems, and suitcases in with the help of parents. Tiffany accompanied me and while most lugged heavy luggage and bulky belongings into the narrow hallway and up the steps, all that belonged to me was what I carried in a large black trash bag. There would be at least two athletes per dorm room, and in some cases the rooms were built for three or more. I wondered whom my roommate would be and if he was already in the room. Soon it was my turn in line, and I provided my first and last name to the assistant coaches who then provided me with my room number.

Tiffany stood by my side as I waited in line for my room keys and once I got my keys she kissed me goodbye, wished me luck, and told me to call her later. I picked up my bag and walked up the steps and as I opened the room door, I was glad to see it was empty and I was the first one there. It was a double and I picked the bed that was closest to the window.

I sat on the bed and looked out the window at the nice view of the campus. I watched parents kiss their sons goodbye and wish them well. At that moment, I wished my mom was around or some other family to celebrate, wish me well, and offer their support. On the brighter side of things, I was in a room that I didn't have to worry about having to leave until I got ready and there wasn't a need to sneak in or out. An hour went by and the entire team was checked in. As luck would have it, the kid that I was supposed to room with never showed up, which meant I would be rooming alone. We reported to the locker room to prepare to be tested in a variety of areas such as bench press, forty-yard dash time, etc. Since I was a transfer student/ freshman, I had not yet been assigned a number so I had no idea what number I would be wearing.

As I entered the crowded locker room, I searched the names above lockers until I finally found mine. Next to my name was the number fourteen. My practice jersey was hanging up in my locker along with other equipment. Testing didn't turn out very well for me in many areas and I was down on myself, but I was careful not to show it in front of others. That evening was hard on me once I was back in my room. I lay in my bed with the windows opened, staring at the full moon. Although I was excited about being at Otterbein and playing football, I was hard on myself with the events earlier that day and I started to question myself. Do I really belong here? How will I compete with the better players? If I fail, would I have to return to the life I knew prior to coming to Otterbein?

My mind was racing and I knew sleep wasn't about to come. I got dressed and left the dorm to take a walk. Not being familiar with the city, I found myself walking all the way to State Street, which was a main street in the city of Westerville. It was around 1:00am and as I was walking I noticed a police cruiser slowly pass me by. Once the officer passed me I looked back at his cruiser and noticed that he had turned in the middle of street and was headed back in my direction. I continued to walk knowing that I was going to be stopped. He pulled up next to me and although it was fully lit on the street, he placed his spotlight on me from the police car and asked where I was going this late.

I was instantly agitated and I replied that I was going to the same place I wanted him to go...to hell. As I continued to walk I heard him exit his car and ask me to stop, he then asked if I had any identification on me. I continued to walk and as I was getting ready to cross the street, another police cruiser pulled right in front of me. I stopped, and as the new officer got out of his car he asked me to place my hands on the hood of his car. I began to curse them both as I was searched and questioned about where I was going. The only witness to what I felt like was harassment were the white folks who slowed as they passed to look at me and shake their heads. Soon, another car was driving by but this time the car stopped and parked.

A tall white guy exited the car and I soon recognized him as one of the assistant coaches. He asked if everything was okay and notified the officers that I was a student athlete at Otterbein, and within minutes the whole attitude of the officers changed. The coach took me back to the dorm and explained to me that during camp I was not allowed to leave the dorm. During the short ride back, he advised me that I needed to be mindful of where I was and although my hometown was just right up the road, this was not the inner city. It was my first of many lessons that I would learn from the Westerville Police Department during my four years at Otterbein.

It wouldn't be too long after camp was over that I would be able to make my way to my home for the next four years. William Henry Fouse was first black student who graduated from Otterbein in 1893. I was allowed to live in the theme house named after him and it was officially named the William H. Fouse House of Black Culture. The HBC, as it would come to be known on campus, was located at the corner of Center Street and Home Street. It was a four-bedroom house with a kitchen, computer lab, living room, TV room, dining room, and a laundry room in the basement.

The house was in great shape compared to what I was accustomed to and it was clear that the home was cared for over the years. As I entered the unlocked door three men who introduced themselves greeted me. Although I was older than them, they were all juniors and seniors who made sure that I would get settled into college life. Mr. Peal had already given them some of my background and I was welcomed into the house with open arms. I was led upstairs to my bedroom to get situated. As I laid my belongings down in the room to observe my new surroundings, it reminded me so much of a prison cell with its size and shape.

The room was big enough just for the twin bed, a small dresser, and a small closet. It was just enough room to move around in and not too much more. Two windows were in the room, one having a clear view of the football field and locker room located directly across the street from the house. For me, the size of the room was not important considering where I had come from so despite its resemblance, I was thankful. I also soon learned it was a much better deal than living in the dorm rooms at the residence halls. Transitioning into my freshman year was an overall learning experience for me. I had to learn how to balance a full course load with playing football.
I had to adjust to living with people who had the same goals, but came from very different backgrounds. It was even a big deal to be reminded that others had support systems in place.

All three of my roommates were members of Alpha Phi Alpha Fraternity, Inc. and my education on the fraternity and Greek life in general would be instant. I watched those brothers and their every move on campus; how they carried themselves, how they dressed, and most importantly, how they were treated. They were very active and involved in other organizations and highly respected not only by other students, but also by faculty and staff. Everyone knew them, and anything happening on campus either involved them or was a result of their work. They drove nice cars, had nice clothes, and were always the life of the party. I respected them in many ways and I took the time to learn about the history of Alpha Phi Alpha on my own.

As I studied the history of the organization, I was also learning about the importance of community service and giving back to my community. During my first quarter after being at my first college party and staying out with them well past 3:00am, these brothers woke up after only a few hours of sleep that Saturday morning to perform community service at a local nursing home. I was a part of that experience and learned that for them, this was normal in terms of giving back. It didn't take long before I came highly interested in Alpha Phi Alpha and just a couple of weeks into the quarter, I saw flyers inviting those men interested in learning more about the organization to attend an informational session.

My roommates didn't speak much to me about Alpha, nor did they encourage me to show up. On the night of the informational, I remember walking out of my room and noticed all of my roommates had on suits and ties. Confused as to where they were going, they were equally confused as to why I was dressed in jeans and a t-shirt headed to this meeting. No one said anything to me and I proceeded to walk across campus to the meeting. When I arrived at the meeting I felt like a fruit loop in a bag of Cheerios. I was out of place in terms of how I was dressed but I stayed anyway. There would be a couple more meetings and the number of people that showed up decreased based on the high GPA requirement for membership.

I also learned that out of all the Black Greek Letter Organizations, Alpha had the highest GPA requirement for its potential members. Many of the gentlemen who were interested members didn't meet the standard, nor would they ever. It quickly became clear that I was interested in Alpha. I continued to do my research on the organization and learn its history. I showed up to the study tables the members hosted which actually helped me to manage my time and improved my study habits. The current members made it very clear to all of the potential members that not graduating and building a legacy of leadership was completely unacceptable. They often asserted that graduating should be our number one priority. That message was clear, and they all led by example by carrying GPAs of 3.0 or better.

As my first quarter came to a close, I was thankful to have worked hard in my classes and was on my way to having a 3.0 GPA. While I can't go into detail as to all of the additional requirements to gain entry into the organization, what I can tell you is that the six other men that went through the process with me will forever carry a strong bond between them. We placed ourselves in situations that allowed our weaknesses to become our strengths and learned lessons in nobility and excellence. We also gained lifelong brotherhood and accountability. Alpha became my school for the making men better, and I was on my way to being a better man because of my affiliation with these men. Gaining membership into Alpha was a rewarding experience for me in undergrad and granted me a certain status on campus and in the community.

To say the least, Alpha instilled in me a sense of ownership and belonging that I never had. Each one of us was given a name upon initiation on March 6, 1999, and it was at this time Lion Heart was introduced to the world. Notice I didn't say that Lion Heart was *born*. I have learned that it has been within me and that I have been calling on the inner strength that the name speaks to all along. Alpha was the conduit that God sent as an outward expression of my inner strength. I'm proud to say that I can travel anywhere in the world and know that I have brothers of Alpha there. During the process of gaining membership, I learned a valuable poem that is near and dear to my heart.

The Man Who Thinks He Can

~Author Unknown

If you think you are beaten, you are If you think you dare not, you don't, If you like to win, but you think you can't It is almost certain you won't.
If you think you'll lose, you've lost For out of the world we find, Success begins with a fellow's will It's all in the state of mind.
If you think you are outclassed, you are

You've got to think high to rise, You've got to be sure of
yourself before You can ever win a prize.
Life's battles don't always go To the stronger or faster man,
But soon or late the man who wins Is the man WHO THINKS
HE CAN!

Initially I had only learned the words, but I soon understood the meaning behind the words that made my life more thematic. The words truly empowered me to believe in my abilities, and gave me the confidence of knowing that no matter what, I can succeed at anything I put my mind to. During some of the toughest times in my life, I have recited this poem and it has served as a constant reminder that if my mind was focused on doing it, then I could achieve it. My Otterbein experience came with many challenges and triumphs. My sociology and criminology coursework came very easy to me. In the beginning I put in very little effort and was still able to pass with at least a B.

I remember in one class we were to give a presentation on a topic, which I had forgotten to complete. I was reminded of it as I was walking to class with a longtime friend and classmate Chasity. She was shocked and somewhat concerned that I had not prepared to give the presentation and jokingly made fun that I was going to get an F. She had put a lot of work into her presentation over the past week, but I looked at her and smiled and told her I would be okay. We soon arrived in class and while others were presenting on their topics, I was reviewing which topic I was going to present. Once I picked my topic, the professor asked who was willing to go next.

I eagerly raised my hand and Chasity's expression of shock was obvious. For the next ten minutes I would go on to give the most powerful presentation of the class on sentence disparities in the criminal justice system and received an A as my grade. The professor gave me major kudos during class on the presentation and had no idea that I had just given what some may call an extemporaneous speech, but Chasity would call it "B.S," especially considering that I scored higher than her on the project.

131

It would not be long before the small class sizes began to tip professors off to my lack of effort. They began to challenge me to think deeper on topics and became more critical of my work. Although I never shared my story in class or in papers, responding to topics based on my own personal experience was something I gave very little to and often times my responses were not enough. Professors started to see right through my smoke and mirrors and encouraged me to be more authentic and analytical. It was not enough to just know one sociological theory and be well versed in it. I was challenged to be able to understand and interpret many of them. I am glad to say that I was successful.

While most students were afraid to stand up in class and speak, I would take introductory and advanced public speaking classes to not only improve my skills, but to learn from other students. I watched and listened to my classmates and picked up some good speaking habits. While some students were taking electives to get by with credits, I would take classes that I was not only interested in, but classes I thought would prepare me for my future. My past struggles with math eventually caught up with me. Because I placed so low in math, I had to take two math courses plus a statistics course. I struggled in those classes but made sure to communicate with my professors daily seeking out additional assistance outside of class, and attending the optional math lab.

I followed the same strategy that helped me to pass at Columbus State. I was able to pass those classes with low B's and C's and I was okay with that. Throughout my entire academic career, I was on the Dean's List twice. By the end of my junior year I admit that I was starting to grow tired of the demands of the coursework and it started to show. This was also the time where I found out my mom was headed back to prison after just recently being released. She was sentenced to carry out the remaining time of her original sentence for violating her parole conditions by committing a new offense.

I had high hopes of her being home, being able to see me play football, but even better, watching me walk across the stage when it was time to graduate from Otterbein. Depression set in and I started to put very little effort into my schoolwork, doing just enough to get by. Attending class every day and on time were no longer priorities for me. I focused more attention on partying on and off campus, and interactions with young ladies. My grades fell from an overall GPA of 3.0, to just under a 2.5, but I was still on pace to graduate. Knowing that I was not going to be seeing my mom for years just didn't sit well with me. One night I decided against going to a party with the rest of my roommates because I was feeling down.

None of them knew that I was struggling as I hid my current heartache from them. When the house was empty, I sat down in the living room and started crying uncontrollably. All the past hurt and pain that I had dealt with was catching up to me. I had tried to shield that pain with school and it was catching up, and completely unavoidable. I ran into the kitchen and pulled out the biggest knife that I could find. I sat back down on the couch and I wanted to end it all right then and there. I placed the tip the knife right over my heart and I had every intention of stabbing myself right where it hurt, right where the pain was.

As I pulled the knife back to stab myself that same voice I heard while I was prison spoke to me in a soft voice, "You should know the plans I have for you. Plans to prosper you and not harm you, but plans to give you hope and future. Continue to believe in me." Those words took away the strength that I was going to use to stab myself to death. I dropped the knife to the floor and continued crying uncontrollably. After I cried my last tear, I picked myself up and walked into my room, never to mention this moment to anyone. Although I still continued to struggle in classes, I did do other things that would end up going a long way after college. I obtained an internship at the Franklin County Work Release Program and I was able to receive credit hours for my time there. They knew that I was an ex-offender but still gave me the opportunity.

While I was there I worked first hand with the inmates doing intake paperwork, assisting with placing them on the house arrest monitoring systems, and doing security checks. I even had the experience of running into my first cousin who was an inmate there at the time. When our eyes met he looked confused. I could tell he was unsure of my status. Was I an inmate or staff? As he approached to speak, my nonverbal communication skills kicked in and I gestured for him to keep it moving and not speak. He gladly obliged and did just that. When we crossed paths again, we would casually speak to each other but kept it moving. I was so grateful for the opportunity and it felt good to begin doing things in my field of study that I could add to my resume.

When I wasn't in the books I kicked it, and kicked it hard. Some of the hardest decisions were about which parties to attend. Being that I was an Alpha also meant that stepping or strolling was involved in just about every party. Although I wasn't known for being a good dancer, I learned how to step and stroll with the rest of my fraternity brothers, and at times I'd even lead a few select strolls around the party. These were primetime moments when the ladies would stop dancing, even if they were dancing with a man, to observe us. We'd often joke that the ladies wanted to be with us, and the fellas wanted to be us.

I loved the attention that being in the spotlight would garner and I used it to my advantage when it came to the interest from young ladies. Where most guys knew they needed to do something to be noticed by ladies or invite them out on dates, most times all we had to do was wink or make eye contact as we passed them. That would almost always result in a conversation or an invitation after the party to grab a bite to eat, or hang out at our house. We'd step just about the whole party and would be soaked in sweat by the time we were done. My status as an Alpha and college football player brought me more attention than I wanted on a few occasions, but most times I welcomed it. Most parties didn't really happen unless we showed up. Not only did we throw some of the best parties on campus, but we also benefited from having Ohio Wesleyan, Capital University, Devry Institute, Ohio Dominican University, Franklin

University, and Columbus College of Art & Design under our charter. We were also sure to support our brothers at nearby Wittenberg University, Denison University, Ohio University, and Ohio State University. So for those of us who were willing to get on the road, there was always something going on.

Because we didn't see eye-to-eye on things that our classmates who were members of white fraternities and sororities did on campus, we often excluded ourselves from their activities. In an effort to build bridges on campus one year, we wanted to solidify relationships and unify our communities. Historically, Greek Week was for just the white fraternities and sororities, but this year we wanted to participate. When a few of the organizations caught wind of this, they strongly disapproved stating that we needed to have our own Greek Week within the black community. It was decided that we would not be participating. As a result, we decided we would secretly teach one of the sororities a step show routine that would enable them to win the talent portion of the competition.

There were strict rules about getting outside help, so my brothers would meet them in rooms we reserved on campus and teach them the routine. On the day of the show, right before they were to go on stage, we entered the campus center about fifteen strong and stood in the crowd in silence. As the ladies began to step, the crowd stood in disbelief. The place erupted with applause while the ladies were on stage stepping and chanting. At the end of their performance, the ladies of Kappa Phi Omega invited our entire chapter on stage to join them in the step. The ladies knew that inviting us on the stage would get them disqualified, but the electricity in the room and statement we were making was bigger than winning.

After that night, things changed for the better between the Black Greek Letter Organizations and the White Greek Letter Organizations. We changed the culture of our campus and created an environment that allowed us to celebrate our differences and learn from each other and serve our community together. Athletically, I excelled on the football field, lettering my sophomore and junior year as a running back. After spending a season and a half on the junior varsity squad, my breakthrough to playing on Saturdays in front of the large crowd came during my sophomore year against Capital University.

I took the opening kickoff back over eighty yards, had seven tackles on special teams, and rushed for nearly one hundred yards in that game. For the first six games of my junior year, I led the conference in kickoff return yardages averaging over nineteen yards per carry. That year I had over five hundred yards in kickoff return yardages and made several monumental plays on special teams that placed us in good positions to win games, and even was ranked nationally for four weeks as the top kickoff returner. Even though I never started in a college game on Saturdays, I always busted my butt on the scout team helping the defense prepare for the upcoming games.

I was well respected on my team and around the conference. Heading into my senior year, I had high expectations for myself to finally get more playing time as a running back or a slot receiver. We were under a new head coach that year that brought in a new offense that I was highly excited about, although from my introduction of him I had a vibe about him that just didn't sit well with me. The summer before camp started, I busted my butt in the weight room and it showed the first day of camp when we were being tested. I reported to camp in the best shape I had been in since coming to play. I was beyond excited when the season started because I was practicing with the second team offense.

I had learned both positions as a running back and slot receiver. That excitement overheard the head coach make comments that were directed towards the black football players on the team. We were commonly referred to as "you people" and would regularly be the punch line to jokes that only white players thought were funny. I was on to him and his remarks and I could see right through him. During any of our interactions I made it clear that I knew that he was racist. Other teammates who were black overlooked the remarks and jokes, but I grew tired of them.

My teammates would encourage me to let it go based on us having to deal with him for only one season. I refused to let it slide. Otterbein was my home and his behavior wasn't welcomed in my home. I had learned that Otterbein wasn't a place where that was tolerated, so I decided to confront him. He and I were off in a secluded area on the practice field during the second week of the season when I decided to speak my mind. I shared that his words and jokes were more offensive than funny, and referring to blacks as "you people" only reinforced our belief that he was racist. He apologized to me and expressed that he never means anything by the words. I walked away from the meeting feeling good that he would commit to changing his behavior.

During the week of the following game, I was reduced back down to the scouting team offense, no longer practicing with the first or second team offense. I was told that they needed me strictly on offense as a running back only to help the defense prepare for games, and I was the best running back that could give the defense good looks. Three and four weeks went by into the season without me seeing the football field outside of my normal roll of returning kicks. I grew frustrated and it showed after each game. During a particular week after practice, one of my white teammates repeated a comment he had heard the coach say and he directed it towards me. It was a comment about blacks eating chicken and watermelon.

Out of anger, I started to rush the guy and was quickly held back by other teammates in the locker room. The head coach soon walked in and approached me. He put his face in mine and asked me what my problem was. By this time the whole locker room had grew quiet with the attention focused on us. I stepped one foot forward towards him and while we looked as if we were squaring off for the next title belt fight, I looked him dead in his eyes and said, "You're my problem you racist bastard!" "What did you just call me?" he replied. "I said you're a racist bastard and everybody on this team knows you are, but nobody is willing to stand up and tell you."

"Call me that again, and your ass if off this team," he yelled. In a final act of defiance I stepped closer. We were almost nose-to-nose at this point and with more emphasis than the previous two times I said, "You're a racist bastard and you don't have to kick me off this team because I quit!" I reported the incident to Dean of Student Affairs, who investigated the situation. The coach was eventually let go after that season and while I don't know whether that incident was the reason for his dismissal, I do know that he didn't display the same values that Otterbein holds near and dear.

I was left feeling empty after not completing the season or my career. Not finishing with the same people I started with my freshman year was hard. I had an opportunity to go back and finish the season, but I felt as if the damage was done on both ends. All of the apologizing in the world could not erase what was deeply rooted in his heart. During the spring, right before graduation, I received a letter that I had been picked to play in a National All-Star game in Cleveland, Ohio. I have no idea how I was picked, but I was. It was an opportunity for me to say goodbye to the game and have that one last opportunity to show my skills. I ended up having the best game of my life. I ended the game with over one hundred all-purpose yards.

I was playing against some of the top players across the country in Division III and I represented Otterbein very well. As a result of my performance, I was then invited to play in another All-Star game in Louisville, Kentucky against even tougher competition. I didn't have the breakout performance I had in the last game, but this game was special as it was the first time I had started in a meaningful football game. I found out that I would be starting right before kickoff, and my energy and adrenaline went through the roof. Just like I did at Otterbein, I took the opening kickoff sixty yards and set the tone for an opening touchdown. Outside of that, my performance was marginal at best as I took a beating every time I touched the ball. I finished the game with twelve yards on five carries. As the clock ran down during the 4th quarter to zero, the realization set in that most athletes eventually face.

This is the end, the last time I will ever suit up to play, the game I have loved since I was able to carry a football. As the tears flowed, I still held my head high knowing that I always did my best. I was blessed to have never been seriously injured, and even more blessed to have been granted all these opportunities to play. I ended the game feeling like a champion. I returned to Ohio with great news that I had been accepted into graduate school at East Tennessee State University majoring in Criminal Justice. I had applied to at least four other schools, but with poor GRE scores and my GPA below a 3.0, none of the schools accepted me. I was very excited about being accepted, however nervous considering I had never lived anywhere outside of Columbus.

Outside of visiting the school one time for an interview for a graduate assistantship, I knew nothing about the city or state. I gladly accepted the offer for the GA position and began to set my mind on moving after the summer. It soon dawned on me during spring quarter that I had lived on Otterbein's campus all year round for the past four years, and the thought of leaving actually made me nervous. In addition, I also realized that I had no place to go after graduation. Otterbein would not allow me to stay on campus after graduation. God had always promised to keep me in his plans, and this time would be no different. I was able to land a Resident Advisor position in the Upward Bound Program at the University of Cincinnati working with high school boys.

They would provide me with room and board and a monthly stipend. It was just the break I needed to get by until I left for graduate school in Tennessee. Weeks before graduation I was approached by the Columbus Dispatch that they wanted to do a cover story on me and my success. They had contacted me my junior year, and I just didn't feel comfortable at the time sharing my story, so I respectfully declined. I didn't feel comfortable with the campus, or even the Westerville community as a whole, knowing my past for fear of being treated differently. I had no idea how the Columbus Dispatch even knew anything about me in the first place.

Still, I was reluctant to share the story until late one night I was on the phone with a young lady that I had cared deeply about. She was the first person I can honestly say had my heart while I was college. We often joked that if we got married she wouldn't have to change her name since it was already Wilson. While I was telling her the reason for my hesitation, she told me something that to this day set the stage for how I viewed myself moving forward. "Rayshawn, you don't realize it now, but God has blessed with you with a gift, and He has plans to use you in so many ways that is going to be a blessing to others."

Her words touched my spirit in a way that had never been done before, and I was left speechless. It was after that phone call that I decided to do the story. A few weeks before graduation I was told that I was picked to be one of the speakers at the ceremony. It was an honor that to this day I still appreciate. Days leading up to graduation were bittersweet for me and filled with a variety of emotions. Packing my belongings was hard and saying goodbye to friends that had become family proved to be too much. Otterbein was home and served as my family and primary support system, something that was nonexistent up until the day I set foot on campus.

It didn't seem real until I received my graduation tickets. I was provided with seven and after a passing them out to a few family members, I was left with just one ticket. Filled with emotions, I cried wishing that I were giving that ticket to my mom. Instead of throwing the ticket away, I sent it to her with a letter that simply said I wish you were here. With the help of Gary, one of my fraternity brothers who was also my roommate and teammate on the football field, his family allowed me to share a graduation party with him.

All I had to do was invite people and they took care of everything else. It was such a kind gesture for his family to allow me to share in such an event. The bonds that Alpha allowed me to establish indeed gave me more than just brothers, it gave me the family that I never had. I'm still grateful to him and his family for making sure I felt celebrated after earning my degree.

The day of graduation was Father's Day 2002. The story that I interviewed for had come out in the *Metro* section and featured a nice photo of me standing next to an Otterbein sign on campus. As I stood in line to march across the campus heading into the gymnasium, I was greeted by several of my professors who had read the article. I was bombarded with hugs and congratulatory statements. One professor approached me in tears and as she hugged me she whispered, "God has taken you this far and He has so much in store for you. Continue to always put your trust in Him."

When it was my turn to walk across the stage, I looked out among the audience to see the majority of the crowd rise to their feet as my name was called. As I shook hands with the President of the college and he placed the diploma in my hand, I immediately felt powerful. For the first time in my life, I felt a sense of accomplishment and it felt awesome. I had no idea what God had in store for me next, but I had my mind set on accomplishing more.

"The hardest work in the world is being without work"
~Whitney M. Young

WHAT I WAS, NOT WHO I AM?

After leaving the security that Otterbein provided, I was on my way to East Tennessee State University. I picked right up where I left off by engaging on campus with my fraternity brothers and making a name for myself as a student who was serious about his education and enjoyed making an impact on the community. It was different though for the reason that I had created a family at Otterbein and it just didn't feel the same to be so far from away from home. However, it was a beautiful campus and the serenity of the mountains was so calming that I wished I could take them with me when I left.

After spending just one year there, homesickness got the best of me and I was back on the road with Columbus on my mind and in my heart. The difference upon my return was clear. I didn't have a room waiting for me at Otterbein and I had to find a job. Real life had just kicked in and I was immediately faced with eating food and living under a roof that wasn't covered by room and board. Despite the many obstacles I had overcome and accomplishments I had under my belt, nothing could have prepared me for the experience of being shot down time after time when it came to employment. It was as if I were a bird soaring in the sky that had flown over an area where hunters were waiting for it.

With each flap of its wings, another shot rang out and the bird was forced to continue flying while dodging attempts to bring it down. Stopping to rest meant a sure death and focusing on where the next shot would come from would only serve as a distraction to the mission of rising and surviving. I was determined to live a respectful and productive life. All of a sudden I felt like I had just been released from prison and realized that each time I filled out an application I was putting myself in a position for someone who knew nothing about my life, my struggles, and my triumph to judge me and determine if I was fit to earn a living doing what I had acquired the skills to do.

I unknowingly made myself a target by labeling myself an ex-offender one based. I would introduce myself to potential employers as an ex-offender searching for employment. In an attempt to be proactive before they would ask about the conviction, I felt it was my duty to bring it up and discuss it first. Despite my transparency and with no work experience, I was turned away from many potential jobs without explanation. My self-esteem, self-worth, and spirituality began to suffer. The weight of not being able to find employment meant that I couldn't continue to pursue my goals and dreams. My girlfriend that I was living with at the time would be frustrated and forced to carry the burden. I couldn't understand why after all I had done to move forward from my past, I was still being forced to suffer consequences from it. Hadn't I been rehabilitated according to the criminal justice system? Hadn't I done enough to show my potential and intentions?

It didn't help that when reading the Sunday paper under the employment section I would see a job that I wanted to apply for only to continue reading and see words that indicated I didn't even need to waste my time applying: "Applicant must successfully pass a background check." These situations began to shape my belief that the society in which I was living did not want folks like me to succeed. That belief was based on the number of barriers and collateral sanctions that I was facing. In addition, I was faced with the painful realization that the number of barriers for men who looked like me were numerous, no matter what we did after release from prison. Since I was unable to secure work in my field of study, I turned my attention to factory and temp service work to make ends meet.

The words "no" and "sorry" or "We'll be in touch" began to feel like punches to my face and I was convinced that some unseen force was dead set on showing me that I should just lay down and stop rising, or head back to the streets where the line of employment is always open for those willing to put in work. While driving home one day I was stopped at the railroad tracks by a train and as I sat there in the car discouraged, I looked to my right and noticed a signed that read "Now Hiring."

The sign was in front of a warehouse that packaged and shipped ice. I turned into the parking lot, grabbed a copy of my resume, and headed up the stairs into the building. Once inside, I greeted the receptionist and asked her for an application. I filled out the application and actually felt good about the possibility until I came across the question that many ex-offenders dread answering: "Have you ever been convicted of a felony?" Lying on applications was never an option for me. I wasn't ashamed of who I was and I also knew that many employers conducted background checks. I wrote down my response, "I pled guilty to theft in 1996." After signing the application, I walked back up to the receptionist who then phoned the hiring manager.

When my name was called, I eagerly jumped from my seat and followed him to his office as he read over my resume and application. I sat quietly watching his eyes and body language. "Oh, I see you went to Otterbein College. Such a fine college!" "Yes sir, I did. I played football there as well." As he continued to scan my application, his demeanor changed once he got to the bottom of the page. "I'm sorry Mr. Wilson, but I don't hire people with felony backgrounds." As he stood up, I stood up and began to plead my case, basically borderline begging him for a job. But he refused to listen, and interjected with very rude and matter of fact comments. "Have a nice day Mr. Wilson."

Each time he said that my frustration grew. I stopped and said, "It's clear that I can do this job. What do you think I'm going to do, steal ice?" He handed me my resume with the application and pointed at the door. Being dismissed like I wasn't a human being was the straw that broke the camel's back. I threw the papers in his direction and told him that he was full of shit as I stormed out the door. The fact that I couldn't even get a job shipping and packing ice with a college degree was more than I could bear. I went home to my girlfriend and cried my eyes out. She provided as many words of encouragement as she could.

I sat down in the basement of the home we shared and began thinking about what I could and needed to do. After all, it became clear that my current strategy was not going to work. I used some of the skills I learned at Otterbein and took to the Internet to research ways to have more impact during an interview. That night I studied and printed off interview questions, watched YouTube videos on how to effectively interview and sell oneself to employers. I found myself still awake at 3:00am looking at videos of how to answer different questions with confidence. Not only did I gain some tools, I learned that I was going about my strategy the wrong way. I needed to regroup and devise a new game plan.

The first task was to learn how to communicate effectively when interviewing. I noticed that with some questions I would stumble through the answer, or it would take me a long time to respond, which came across to some employers as a lack of confidence in my abilities or myself. Many of the interview questions were basically the same, just worded differently. I thought back to my college course work and the public speaking classes in which I excelled. I realized that I had to use those same techniques and transfer them to interviewing. I studied the interview questions before drafting my answers and committing them to memory.

I created my own scenarios so when employers asked me the behavioral interview questions, I would be prepared. I connected with friends and professionals who would take me through mock interviews and provide me with critical feedback. From there I developed a new strategy for interviewing. I would go into interviews selling myself from every angle that I could. Areas where I lacked experience I would augment with character and leadership skills. Once I felt like I had sufficiently sold myself, I would strategically bring up the felony and why it should be seen as an asset to companies as opposed to a liability and why I was still the best person for the position. I also learned that at the end of the interview, I needed to ask a few questions that would demonstrate that I had done my due diligence to research the company.

The initial implementation of my new strategy would come while interviewing at Alvis House Inc., a well-known organization within the state of Ohio that operated several halfway houses. I was interviewing for a Corrections Specialist position, which is essentially a position of monitoring client's behavior and whereabouts. The position was paying only ten dollars an hour, but it was in my field of study and I was excited. After interviewing with human resources, she sent me down to the facility to meet the manager, and then I was to meet with the CEO and COO.

The whole interview process was going well until I met with the CEO and COO. During our meeting, the CEO informed me that he would not hire me because of the felony conviction. I pleaded with the CEO to give me a shot and he continued to shake his head no, and asked the COO to walk me out. I gathered my things and myself and I walked out of the office. Just before I crossed the threshold of the front door, the COO stopped me, provided me with her card and said, "Mr. Wilson, please continue to be in touch with me. I truly believe you have a bright future." I took Denise Robinson's card and extended my hand to shake hers. She grabbed my hand and proceeded to wrap her arms around me in an encouraging embrace.

She asked me to promise her that I would stay in touch and I did without hesitation. During my job search, I began to notice that potential employers would conduct a background check and then base their employment decisions on my original charges as opposed to what I pled guilty to. On paper and in reality, aggravated robbery and the felonious assault are a lot more violent in comparison to theft. I felt like I was suffering from double jeopardy and the original charges came across to employers like I was some type of hard-core, violent criminal. Some employers even had a list of disqualifying offenses that would make it impossible to be considered for employment.

It didn't take long to realize that my offense was never on those lists, and at times in the interview when I felt it was appropriate, I would simply ask, "Are you not hiring me because you have policies and procedures stating that you don't hire ex-offenders with my conviction, or are you simply just choosing not to for no rhyme or reason? Particularly considering that my conviction is not a disqualifying offense of your agency?"

To some, this would come off rather unwise and counterproductive, but this was my way of saying that I was not a dummy, and even if you won't hire me I'll leave here with my dignity and respect intact. My line of questioning was also my way of challenging employers to take into account the nature and gravity of the offense, the time that has passed since my conviction and subsequent release, and the nature of the position in which they were seeking to fill. Additionally, I wanted employers to think about those questions so when the next ex-offender came in to apply, it would encourage them to be more open-minded and generate some discussion. There's never been a time where I applied for a job where my skills didn't match the position.

In some cases, my experience would surely enhance my ability to do the job. After a few failed attempts, my hard work would finally pay off when I interviewed at Columbus State Community College for an Academic Advisor position with the Upward Bound Program. I came into the interview as prepared as I could be and I had the confidence to match. I made it a point to sell myself, and even expressed that I was best person for the job. By the time it came down to discussing my felony, I made it hard for them to tell me no, and the lady was willing to bend over backwards to offer me the position. It also helped that I had two fraternity brothers working in that department as well.

They were able to serve as character references for me in addition to another friend's mother. In the end, it was a great relief and sense of accomplishment to get the job. Those folks who said a kind word and thought enough of me to give me an opportunity don't realize what it meant to me to land a job in a field that required me to use my degree. This possibility allowed me to be proud of who I was and what I had been through. I was equally excited to be in a position to impact the lives of the high school students that I would be assisting. The symbolism wasn't lost on me either. Once I was released from prison, I had enrolled at Columbus State to begin taking college courses.

Now I would be employed there and walk the campus as a professional, not an ex-offender.

During my year and a half there, I obtained my masters degree in Criminal Justice Administration at Tiffin University. It took me one year to complete that program by attending class each Saturday from 8am-8pm. During that year, I focused just about all of my attention and research on the topic of re-entry of an ex-offender into the general population. I studied hundreds of journal articles to understand the concept of re-entry, what works, and what doesn't work in providing evidence-based practices with the ex-offender population.

Every paper I wrote was something related to re-entry and ex- offenders, even the scholarly project I developed was based on re- entry. I designed a course to educate people on all aspects of re- entry and how to best work the ex-offender population. Although I was armed with this advanced degree, I was still faced with challenges regarding employment with certain agencies due to my felony conviction. It was clear that interviewing was not always going to be enough and after talking to a few people in the community, I realized that it's not about what or who you know, but who knows you.

This was a very different mindset from what I was always taught. In turn, I took heed and knew I would have to find a way to get people to know me, and most important, to trust me. Since I felt that I was well- rounded in the area of re-entry, I came up with the idea of becoming an entrepreneur and I would promote myself as a re-entry and ex- offender consultant. I was able to print very cheap business cards, acquired a P.O. Box under my business name, created my own letterhead, and pulled a logo off of the Internet that matched the company name. In my quest of finding a way to get noticed, I discovered a number of criminal justice conferences that would take place in Central Ohio that I thought would be beneficial to attend. I knew these conferences would be an opportunity for me to meet people and begin the process of introducing myself to the public.

Quite honestly, I couldn't afford these conferences but I put on the only suit I owned, filled my briefcase with copies of my resume, business cards, and the re-entry curriculum that I developed and walked into these conferences as if I belonged there. I would go to the registration table and tell them I had lost my badge and request a blank one to write my name on. The subjects covered during the different breakout sessions would be outside of the rooms, and I would pick sessions that I was knowledgeable about or had interest in and walk in like I belonged there.

Once inside, I would listen and when it was time for Q &A, I was intentional and deliberate about chiming in on discussions and bringing up additional questions that challenged people to think more critically about a particular subject. I made a concerted effort to show my knowledge & understanding of the subject matter. I was always certain to raise the notion of directly asking ex-offenders what they wanted from the community once they were released, and to communicate that they were expected to contribute to society. I would also identify myself as an ex-offender and a consultant on all things concerning re-entry.

If time permitted, I would briefly share my academic credentials and relevant statistics that I memorized from past research. It was my way of presenting myself as an expert in the field. By the time the sessions were over, I always had a few people waiting to speak with me. Hook, line, and sinker, we would exchange contact information and agree to do lunch or get together for a meeting. I would continue mixing and mingling with people and walk my way right in with the others for lunch. I would wait for people to sit down before I would find an open seat and have lunch before attending the afternoon sessions. Several times a year in various cities, I would attend these conferences and follow-up with people through letters and emails. During those lunches, I found myself taking a genuine interest in those who were around the table and learn as much as I could about their careers. My ultimate goal was to gain insight on how I should maneuver professionally.

These individual and group encounters sometimes led to small contracts and training opportunities. My biggest lunch meeting came when I had the opportunity to meet Mrs. Yvette McGee Brown, former Franklin County Domestic Court Judge before becoming the first African-American female justice on the Ohio Supreme Court. To this day, I'm not sure how I came in contact with her and was able to schedule lunch with her, but it would prove to be life-changing. She knew my story and even had my younger brother in her courtroom when she served as judge. During our conversation, she asked me about the places in which I had been applying and interviewing.

I provided her with that laundry list and included the most recent application to be a juvenile probation officer. This was my ideal job and my interest, excitement, and passion were all about to line up if I could just land the job. Mrs. Brown explained that she doesn't put her name out there for just anyone, but sees the potential in me and suggested that I remain in contact with her. Within an hour of me returning home from lunch, I received a call from the Probation Department setting me up with an interview the following day. I later learned that over one hundred people had applied for the two open positions, and I was one of the two chosen.

It was interesting for me to be on the other side of the criminal justice system where my primary goal in community corrections was to protect the community by managing adolescents who were adjudicated of either a misdemeanor or felony. This was my first inside look on the other side of a system that I was once a part of. The overall experience of working there paved the way and opened doors to further opportunities, but what I witnessed was disheartening. Although the kids needed to be held accountable for their actions, the way they were treated during the process was eye- opening. I witnessed first-hand the way racism still plays a part in decisions, policies, and procedures. I spent a lot of time in the courtrooms and witnessed how deals were made with the prosecutor and judges that determined the fate of children prior to them even having showed up to court.

These children were ordered to complete programs at agencies that were not culturally competent, nor were they equipped to serve the population they were being paid to serve. A lack of cultural competence always led to frustration on the juvenile's part, which would lead to them not showing up and failing to comply with a court order. Once they didn't comply, probation was revoked and it was only a matter of time before they were sent to the Ohio Department of Youth Services for at least six months and in some cases, until their 21st birthday.

The kids had no idea how the juvenile system was preparing them for the adult system when we had to start collecting their DNA to be stored in a database, so if they ever committed a crime their DNA would be left behind. The position was sometimes a dangerous one and posed some challenges. I was often supervising kids whose parents I knew from my childhood. Being connected in a sense, both because of my past and knowing the parents, made it a bit awkward for me to stand up in front of the judge and make a recommendation for the child to be sent to prison. My life was often threatened and people who knew me prior to leaving prison viewed me as the enemy and often treated me like I was the police when they saw me in the community.

Working as a probation officer gave me the opportunity in the courtroom to either be part of the prosecution team or the defense team, depending on my recommendations when kids were being seen for a probation violation. The judges would strongly consider our recommendations since we worked so closely with the youth. In the beginning, it was hard for me to stand up and make recommendations for a kid to be sent to prison despite the numerous opportunities they were given to comply and do the right thing. The longer I was in that position, my thought process changed, and I was able to operate with little to no emotion. I once had a moment that was the source of reflection while watching one young man be escorted off to detention after I made the recommendation. I knew that I had just saved his life because he was on a path to destruction and death.

151

I immediately wondered if anyone ever looked at me during my adolescence and had similar thoughts. Over the course of my time as a probation officer and while moving forward in my career, I found myself hiding the fact that I was an ex-offender, or at least not being as open with it as I used to. I never mentioned it to any of my colleagues for fear of being looked at or treated differently while working in the criminal justice field. It was my way of wanting to fit in. I started to keep my story closer to my chest and share on a need-to-know basis. I was attempting to change my identity as well as how I viewed myself.

Society would no longer get to determine who I was. This identify transformation meant that I would no longer speak in public arenas on behalf of ex-offenders. In doing so, I realized that there were tons of other successful ex-offenders who had the same thought process. It was like a secret society of ex-offenders who kept our acknowledgement of each other to a head nod in public, note comparison, and words of encouragement when in private settings. For me, it was all about being accepted into mainstream society and trying to put as much of the past behind me as I could. At the same time, I was also being criticized by struggling ex-offenders due to turning down a few opportunities to do speaking engagements of sharing my story and providing advice.

Any contact with them or help was done on an individual basis behind closed doors. I would spend nearly two years as a probation officer when my next big break came. Denise Robinson from the Alvis House was now the CEO, and she signed off on the approval for me to be hired in my first management position overseeing one of their twenty-five bed facilities. This was the same company in which I had previously been denied employment about three years prior. Working with the population of ex-offenders who had mental health and substance abuse problems, I realized that there were very few African- American males who had a counseling license. It sparked so much interest, that I decided to go back to school to obtain another master's degree in Community Counseling.

After graduating in 2008 from the University of Dayton, I successfully passed the state exam and became a professional counselor in the state of Ohio. Having those extra credentials behind my name started to provide me endless opportunities. Even though in every job interview I still had to explain the felony conviction, my education and credentials were considered a huge asset to organizations. Getting hired soon became nonissue. Even though I could see breakthroughs happening, I still felt as if I could do more and as if I needed to prove myself to society. After passing the state exam, it meant that I was now eligible to be in private practice.

With the help from "Mo," one my frat brothers and close friends who provided me with office space for very little rent, I began providing counseling services and seeing clients. Clients who suffered from addiction, depression, or phase of life issues were the primary clients I would see. Having my own business was a way of creating my own opportunities so that I would not have to depend on someone deciding to hire me ever again. The practice grew into more than my seeing clients. I expanded and began conducting trainings for agencies, administering assessments for the courts, and ultimately starting my own Driver Intervention Program for those individuals convicted of DUIs.

Although I was knee deep in providing mental health services, I still had a passion for the criminal justice system and re-entry with ex- offenders and often found myself at my happiest when I was working with them. The biggest opportunity that really solidified my place in the community was a call I received one day from a close friend of mine name Tei. At that time, Tei worked for the Department of Education in the Mayor's office. She called me asking for a favor, stating that the Mayor wanted to do something involving re-entry work and ex- offenders, but his staff was not sure how to proceed and wanted me to come in the next day and speak to his staff. Very excited about the opportunity, I agreed to come in and answer any questions they had.

The meeting would be life-changing for me as I was asked to be the lead re-entry consultant for the City of Columbus and tasked to provide recommendations on how best to serve this particular population. With the help of my frat brother Mo and his company RAMA Consulting Group, I delivered a six-month project that included research on a city, state, and national level, focus groups with service providers and ex-offenders, and compiled all of the information to present my conclusions to the Mayor and his top level staff.

Although the city never implemented my recommendations due to budget restrictions, it still provided me with great exposure in the community, and I was able to build long-lasting relationships with many people in the community. Despite the countless doors of employment that continued to shut periodically with no real chance of walking through them, I have to admit that my conviction has not stopped me from doing what I want to do in life. For every door that closed, God opened additional doors that created other opportunities for employment.

The roles and career moves that I thought I was interested in but wouldn't work out in my favor, turned out to be doing me a favor. I continue to be very fortunate and blessed. I have had so many people that believed in me step up to the plate and advocate for me by making phone calls, sending emails, having meeting, and offering words of encouragement. I have not arrived at the point where I can say I've made it, but where I am is exactly where I'm supposed to be, and I know I didn't get here alone. An ex-offender is a very small part of what I used to be, but it never did, and it never will define who I am.

"Like grief, hope hides, pounces, and taunts, and never leaves." ~Author Unknown

EX-pungement

While working as a Juvenile Probation Officer in the same county where I had once been a youth offender, I reached out to one of my fraternity brothers who operated his own law office. My inquiry was steeped in curiosity about the record expungement process. With all that I had overcome and the path that I knew I was on for my life and my career, it was the next logical step. I was excited at the thought of having my legal past and all that it represented being wiped away. After careful review of my case, his thoughts were that I had a fighting chance even though I didn't fall within the State of Ohio guidelines. Those guidelines stated that one offense could be expunged.

I had two separate offenses even though those offenses occurred within a very short time frame. I still remained hopeful that this would work out in my favor. For the first time in my life, I had someone affiliated with the law and the criminal justice system that believed in me, and that alone was a blessing. Not only did he believe in me, but he also volunteered his time and services to my cause. It was like I could feel the scales that once fell out of my favor begin tipping in my direction. I learned that the expungement request was to be heard in front of Judge David Fias, who was also a graduate of Otterbein College.

Prior to the date of the hearing, there were a few different occasions where I found myself sharing an elevator with the prosecuting attorney who handled my case. She had no idea who I was but I would always catch her looking at my name badge, and I would then watch her mind race as she attempted to search her mental database and make a name to face connection. My response was always the same, which was to make sure she knew that I saw her and without words try to create an expression that said, "You may not remember me, but I'll never forget you." Most times it would just be an intentional, but non-threatening and matter of fact stare followed by a small smirk

For once in my life I was looking forward to going to court and with each postponement, my anxiety grew higher. Just thinking about what I would say, the outcome, and all that it meant to me kept me on edge and I began to grow worried that the day would never come. Just when I thought I couldn't wait any longer, the day had come. I was in the lobby outside of the courtroom standing with my wife and about ten of my closest friends and supporters. Things seemed to move in slow motion as the prosecutor walked by me with a file in hand. I soon found out that the file was mine.

I recognized that it was my file because I had committed the case numbers to memory during my legal research: 95CR9322 and 95CR9323. Prior to entering the courtroom, the prosecutor stopped in front of me and said, "I'm so proud of all the things that you have accomplished. You've done so much and I wish you the best of the luck moving forward." So many emotions ran through my mind after hearing her words. I really didn't know how to take the remarks or how to respond to her.

As we all moved into the courtroom, I took my place at the defendant's table next to my attorney. Being in the same courtroom at the same table where I stood and pled guilty to a crime I didn't commit, standing before the same judge, and the same prosecutor while asking them to basically forgive me for something that I didn't do was a haunting feeling. Only this time, I didn't feel sick to my stomach, nor did I feel like my legs would give out. I felt confident. I felt like I had grown into a man worthy of standing there in that courtroom and humbly demanding respect and an opportunity to correct the past.

The judge allowed my attorney to begin pleading the case and detailing why expungement should be granted. The first order of business was to qualify me for the process even though there were two charges. My attorney stated that the other misdemeanor offense in which I pled guilty during the same timeframe was very close and I was sentenced on the same day. As he stood on my behalf and delivered words that I wished I could have said myself, I focused my attention on the judge and the prosecutor.

My eyes were fixed on the judge's reaction, and then I would glance over and look at the prosecutor gauging the same. She looked on with a slight smirk on her face. My attorney then continued by detailing all of my accomplishments since being released back in 1997. As he navigated through my list of achievements, I noticed my former public defender Scott Wiseman come into the courtroom and take a seat. As we made eye contact, he gave a slight nod indicating that I had his support too. The prosecutor's rebuttal on behalf of the state was very brief and to the point.

She came from behind the table and stood in the middle of the courtroom and made it clear to me, my supporters, and to the judge that I simply did not meet the state requirements to get my record expunged. She went on to say that if the judge did grant the expungement she would appeal to the higher court and more than likely win. Her words began to shatter my reality and my confidence left the courtroom. I felt the scales begin to tip out of my favor once again. I glanced back up at the judge and saw him shaking his head in disbelief, and at that moment I knew it couldn't be good. He then interrupted the prosecutor and said, "The court can do basically what we want to do in this case, you're just choosing not to."

After a few back and forth exchanges, the judge paused for what seemed like forever as he looked over a few papers in front of him. The courtroom grew so silent that despite being up eighteen stories high, I could still hear the traffic from below. He then turned to me and gave me what felt like a life sentence when he said, "Mr. Wilson it has been a very, very long time since I have seen such a success story. I have had the opportunity to read the Columbus Dispatch article and other letters of support by some of whom are here today.

It is very unfortunate Mr. Wilson, but if I grant you this decision it will be short-lived because the prosecutor has made it very clear on what the State intends to do." With each word after what was said I just felt as if my whole world had come crashing down on me.

He further stated that he was not going to rule one way or the other, but would leave it open for future consideration. He encouraged me to continue to do what I was doing in the community. As people started to leave the courtroom, I couldn't feel my feet. I wanted to get up but I just couldn't. I sat looking at the empty bench as the judge left and in that moment I relived the events from my first day of incarceration, to release, and to this present moment. The feelings were too much to keep bottled up and I soon found my head in my hands again, crying uncontrollably. I had paid my debt to society in many ways and had far exceeded the expectations of an ex-offender in terms of my accomplishments. To a large degree, I felt entitled to the opportunity to start all over again.

Instead, I was left feeling empty as if the doors for moving forward were just slammed shut in my face. As the courtroom emptied, the loss of sensation traveled upward to my legs, my head grew heavier, and I simply put my head down on the table and continued to cry. Before long, the courtroom was empty and as I raised my head up in an attempt to regain my composure, I noticed that the judge had reentered and was again sitting at his bench. "Off the record Mr. Wilson, please remain in contact with me. Sometime in the future, please reach back out to me so I can see if there is a way that I can help you. I nodded my head, slowly pushed myself from the table, and stood. I took notice of the image of the scales of justice and although the picture has them balanced, I was sure that at that moment they were not. I walked out of the courtroom feeling defeated, at least for the time being...

The law has since changed in the state of Ohio, making it easier for thousands of people to get their records expunged. In 2012, Senate Bill 337 was passed changing the terminology from "first time offender" to "eligible offenders". Under the new law, an individual is now eligible to get their record expunged if they meet the following criteria: 1) one felony conviction, 2) one misdemeanor conviction, 3) one felony conviction and one misdemeanor conviction even if they are not related to the same case, 4) two misdemeanor convictions even if they are not related to the same case. As under the previous law, convictions for minor misdemeanors, including most non-serious traffic offenses do not count as conviction.

Further, 2-3 convictions related to the same case are considered as one conviction. I remember the excitement that came as I first read the new law, only to read the next portion and find out that I still didn't qualify. Every time I think about the fact that I will never qualify, I grow disappointed, frustrated, and somewhat defeated. I usually reflect back to that day that I decided to steal some batteries out of Kroger's and was charged with a misdemeanor. I was given time served while I was in the county awaiting for my trial. It's crazy to come to terms with something that meaningless costing me a lifetime of pain.

I can't even recall what the hell I needed the batteries for. However, I am delighted to see that thousands of other people will now be released from the bondage of their pasts. As a result of this change in the legal language, thousands of people will be able to get jobs and provide for their families. They will be able to shake off that stigma of being an ex-offender and not have to worry about filling out an application and answering that dreaded question, "Have you ever been convicted of a felony?"
It appears that not much attention has been given to the new law in that many people who are eligible don't even know it. During every speaking engagement, whether I have an audience of two or two thousand, I make sure to dedicate a portion of my remarks to educating my audience on the specifics of this law so that they too can spread the word and someone else can be set free. I've found it therapeutic in dealing with my own situation to empower others, and every time a person says thank you for the new information, or seeks expungement after our interaction, I'm freed just a little bit more.

"While we teach our children all about life, our children teach us what life is all about."
~Author Unknown

FATHERHOOD

I grew up knowing more about my favorite athlete than I did about my own father. Aside from knowing things about a complete stranger after a brief introduction, my knowledge of him was almost non-existent. The vague visual of his physical appearance is a mix of memory and hopeful visualizations I had as a child. John E. Wilson was born somewhere in Texas and moved to California where he met my mother when they worked cleaning homes in Hollywood. Curiosity occupied the place that I wished was full of memories and interactions. Who was he? What was he like? Did he enjoy the time we spent together during my first days on earth?

What would life be like if he were present? None of those questions would ever be answered, and as a matter of fact, the information that I did get about him would only cause more curiosity and questions. The only picture I ever remember of him I ripped up when I was eleven or twelve. I remember being angry one day at my mom for not showing up to a baseball game. All of the other kids had their parents there, mainly their fathers. We lost that game after I struck out with two people on base. I remember being in my bedroom and getting more upset as I sat and looked at the picture of the man I grew up knowing as my father. The only place he existed in my life was on that piece of paper. After I ripped it up, he no longer existed even there.

I received word during my junior year in high school that John had passed away. An aunt who still lived in California casually shared the news that he was an alcoholic, and it was rumored that he had contracted AIDS. No one in my family had any contact with him or any of his family, so I was unsure of where the information could have come from. In the back of my mind I hoped that it was just a rumor that would one day be proven false I remember that after I was off the phone with my aunt discussing his passing, I cried all of 5 minutes and went on with my life as usual. Although I had grown accustomed to existing without a father, his absence never stopped hurting and my pain would intensify when I would see other kids leave sporting events with their dads. I would wonder what it was about me that made him not want to be in my life, and at some point the ever-present pain would cause me to go numb.

Unknowingly, out of the desire to have a meaningful relationship with a father figure, I would latch onto the opportunity to connect with anyone who was willing. Unfortunately for me, some of the men who were willing didn't provide anything close to a positive role model. There was no one to teach me how to throw a tight spiral with the football I carried around, no one to teach me how to stand up in the rest room and pee straight or clean up after myself when I didn't, and more important, no one to teach me how to treat and interact with young ladies. The absence of my father cannot be the sole reason that I have made so many mistakes in my life, but I'm certain that a few of my missteps, particularly when it comes to women, would have been prevented if he were around.

I learned about male/female relationships on the playground. I learned about sex by having sex. I learned how responsible men conduct themselves and take care of their families by doing the total opposite. There were no positive male role models in my family as very few people in my family were even married, and so many people in my family were not even raised by their actual parents or in a two-parent household. Needless to say, I made many mistakes along the way, and my experience would continue to be marred by mistakes that were deeply rooted in not having the guidance that a boy needs to grow into a young man.

A young man needs to transition to a man, and a man needs to be responsible, present, and committed. As I revisited and examined what I did know of my family tree, the limbs reserved for my paternal family were consistently empty. When I look at my family tree, it appears that most of them suffered from absentee fatherhood, incest, their mother was not always around, and my experience was also shared by my younger brother who lacks any relationship with his father outside of knowing his name.

When it came to girls and sex, I was conditioned and led to believe that it was my duty to go out and have sexual relations with as many girls as possible. My very first sexual experience was more of a conquest than anything to do with emotional connections or love. She was hiding during a game of "hide and go get it," and I had found that her and the physical act of grinding my body against hers was my reward. The conquest was celebrated among my circle of friends and would continue to be through all of my adolescent and early adult years. Some of the most gratifying times during my childhood were when I had access to money through my activities in the dope game, and sex was something I could have whenever I wanted it. To me, money was power, and power meant I could have any woman I wanted.

The release and escape sex provided was as close to being high that I would ever get, and like the addicts I sold drugs to, I would spend quite a bit of my time chasing that high at all costs, not once thinking that I could possibly suffer any consequences. The after effects of my actions hardly ever came to mind. Sexually transmitted diseases were possible, but I thought I was invincible. Pregnancy was also a possibility, but I selfishly never even considered what would happen if any of them had gotten pregnant. It was like nothing mattered at those moments except the pleasure I received, and the pleasure I gave.

In my mind, abortions were always an option in my adolescence and through early adulthood. The impact of those abortions I'm sure the women carry around with them to this day. Around the same time that I heard my father had died, I met a girl named Holly who baby-sat in the apartments in which I lived. She was my age and had a head of beautiful blonde hair with a beautiful personality to match. We shared words and almost involuntarily connected in such a way that it made the sex comparable to breathing. Two to three times a week we would be at it, having unprotected sex on a schedule like most would eat meals.

We were so reckless that it was inevitable that something would happen that neither of us wanted. During that same time, my focus was on making as much money as I could in the streets, not caring enough about myself to make good decisions. Therefore, the possibility that I could care about Holly, her feelings, or her well-being were slim to none. I treated her like I had learned to treat everyone else in my life: I was only interested in the relationship for how I could benefit from it. I would regularly use her for money, her car, meals, and anything else I wanted that she could provide. After months of being reckless, she approached me in tears. The words that followed didn't faze me but it was clear that she was affected, "I'm pregnant."

I was oblivious to her words and couldn't conceptualize that I was responsible for bringing a life into the world. I didn't go out of my way to see or have any contact with Holly during the pregnancy, and that was a drastic change because I used to make sure that we saw each other when she had something I wanted. She knew she was being avoided and resolved to let me be who I was. I was caught up in the lifestyle that valued how much I could gain from people's pain, and in order to be successful I had to have an "I don't give a fuck" attitude. That same attitude spilled over into an area that I should have cared about the most, especially considering how I grew up.

My pager went off and it was an alert from Holly attempting to tell me that our daughter was about to be born. I disregarded the page and rolled back over to finish the conquest of another willing female participant. That day in August of 1994, the most beautiful little girl I had ever seen was born. Aside from seeing her when Holly would bring her to my apartment, my interaction with her was nonexistent. I didn't buy diapers or milk, I didn't go to doctor's appointments, I didn't wake up in the middle of the night to feed her. I never heard her first words, nor witnessed her first steps. I had only participated in creating her.

Sadly, her mother and I continued to have sex and it wasn't long before she was pregnant again. July of 1995 would usher a little boy into the world that was in no better of a situation than his sister as it relates to having an active father. On the day of his birth I remember being at my apartment studying to take the math proficiency test that had stopped me from graduating high school. This was also around the same time period that the robbery and stabbing occurred at the Swifty gas station that I was accused of committing. That was indeed a fateful day.

When I reflect on it, I can't help but think that if I were where I should have been that day, my life would have been on a different course. He was only a few months old when I was sentenced to two years in prison, and I couldn't help but be saddened when I finally realized he would have less early memories of his father than I had of mine. I wrote Holly from the inside to ask about the kids and request pictures of them, but by this time I had ruined any possibility of having a real relationship with my children. I had mistreated her, used her, been totally selfish, and all but discarded my own children.

Once the lifestyle I lived caught up with me, with my mind and time occupied by thoughts of the outside world, I grew very remorseful and curious about how the kids were doing. In an effort to get me to leave her alone, she wrote to tell me that the kids were not mine and asked that I leave her alone. Continuous attempts to phone were met with resistance and my calls were never accepted. Despite her letters telling me that I wasn't the father of her children, I knew in my heart that I was, and I thought about them often. Upon my release I was faced with a decision. I could attempt to reconnect with Holly and try to be a part of their lives, or I could focus my efforts on making myself better and establishing a life that would allow them to be proud of me when I was in a position to correct the past.

I opted for the second option. Months went by, which turned into years, and somehow it became easier to act like I didn't know that on the other side of town there were two kids growing up without their father. The harm I was doing seemed to be easy for me to detach from, in spite of the hurt I felt as a child from both my mom and dad. I can only look back and accredit it to the feelings of pride, foolishness, and delayed adolescence brought on by the sense of accomplishment that came when I set foot on the campus of Otterbein College. I had gone from homeless convict, to college football player and big man on campus.

During my second year on campus I managed to make a name for myself on the football field as well as in social circles, and meeting ladies who were interested in me and were willing to give me attention was at an all-time high. One particular young lady caught my eye at a college fraternity party and from the moment we laid eyes on each other, the chemistry was undeniable. Like most of the women in my past, I wasn't interested in an emotional connection. I just wanted to conquer her and put myself in a position to have sex with her whenever I wanted.

Surprisingly, outside of the bedroom, we seemed to enjoy each other's company and often spent time together. I started to like her for more than what we did in the bedroom and before I knew it, she was telling me that she was pregnant. By this time in my development, I had a different outlook on fatherhood. I had friends in college who had children and they embraced fatherhood; therefore, so would I. My excitement grew and although I was in college with limited resources, I would find a way to be a good father this time around. Once football season ended for the year, I landed a work-study job on campus along with a part time job. For the first time in my life I felt good when I thought about bringing a life into this world, and I had a bank account that allowed me to save money. I even learned that it was important for me to care for and be there for the mother of my child.

I accompanied her to medical checkups and did things I thought would make her feel better when she wasn't feeling well. The year 2000 was when another little beautiful girl came on the scene and I was sure to be present for her arrival. As I stood in the delivery room waiting to cut the umbilical cord, I only wished that that was not my first time having that experience. But because it *was* my first experience, I was determined not to miss a single thing and to do everything right. That meant making sure I was fully committed and responsible. I remember thinking that it was a big deal for me to sign the birth certificate so that she would never have to wonder who her father was.

The first few months were hectic on me because of my course load and jobs, but it didn't matter. I was doing what I knew was right and at some point it became second nature to put her first. My family was excited for me and it was a joy I had never experienced to watch my mother smile and play with her. I could feel a change in the man I was becoming. My relationship with the mother and my little girl would take a sudden turn when I began to hear rumors that I may not be the actual father of this little girl, my daughter. I was filled with disbelief and confusion. I didn't want to believe that. She was my daughter whom I had been there for, and to hear that there was a possibility she could not be mine was devastating.

When I questioned her mother about the rumor, the lies she told me raised further speculation. In spite of her screaming, shouting, crying, and best efforts to convince me that I was her father, I demanded a DNA test. After a few months of back and forth, the DNA test was conducted and shortly thereafter I received the certified letter from FedEx that contained the results. As I slowly pulled the perforated edges from the top of the package, my mind raced and my stomach knotted up. All of the medical language was very confusing as I began to read the letter, so I skipped to the numbers at the bottom of the second page of the report. The numbers indicated that there was 99.9% probability that I was not the father.

My heart dropped to the knots in my stomach and tears fell from my eyes. I was so disappointed, so hurt, so angry. Word quickly spread throughout my house and among my roommates. They were all pretty supportive, but nothing could prepare me to share the news with my mother. She knew of my lack of relationship with my two other kids, whom she never knew, and was excited to be a grandmother at the time. To watch the tears fall from her eyes because of the pain hurt me even more. I was also faced with the dilemma of determining how I would now treat this relationship with the little girl I had come to know as my daughter. By this time, she wasn't quite a year old, but she knew who I was and I had grown quite attached to her. There were so many questions that I had to ask and answer.

Could I just walk away from this little girl because of something that wasn't her fault? Was it fair for me to take care of a child that wasn't mine, when I wasn't taking care of the ones that are mine? So many people in my life had opinions about what I should do and it was all very difficult to sort through. The mother swore that the test results were wrong and begged me to believe that I was the only man she had been with at the time. The hurt she had caused me was too deep to overcome and I began to gradually pull away and ultimately stopped being involved in the life of the little girl.

I also thought that the actual father deserved to know he had a pretty little girl, and that pretty little girl deserved to know who her real father was. I was not okay with pretending. The whole ordeal affected me and the hurt spilled over into my academic performance. Already having trust issues with women, this situation further enhanced those issues and lack of respect that I had and displayed for women. I also couldn't help but think about Holly and my two actual children. What I had learned about fatherhood made it impossible for me to continue living without reaching out to her and attempting to right my wrongs. After numerous attempts, Holly refused to even hear me out and wanted nothing of my involvement. I was now once again forced to focus on my current situation. Meaning, I was determined to be the best college student athlete I could be with the hopes of making sure that my present and future did not at all resemble my past.

When I saw the little girl and her mother out shopping once when she was a toddler, she still called me Daddy and it took me by surprise. It was clear at that moment that that little girl was in for a world of confusion and hurt that I was all too familiar with. More than a decade later I would see her every now and then in passing. I can see her coming from a mile away and will never forget her face. The good thing is that she wouldn't know me if I were standing next to her at the bus stop. Her mother still insists that the test was wrong and has even gone so far as to ask if I was interested in taking another test.

My response is always one that allows her to be content living that fallacy, while encouraging her to think about her daughter and what price she will pay for being denied the truth. She still carries my last name and I have no idea of what kind of explanation she gives her daughter about who her father is, or when it's pointed out that her last name is different from everyone else's. In recent years, the conversation about the DNA test has not come up. Despite my lack of trust with her, I have still managed to communicate with her quite often and see her out. Although I'm friendly to her, I will never forget that day when it was confirmed that the little girl was not mine, and although I feel bad for the little girl, I don't regret my decision to walk away.

Years would go by without even the slightest amount contact with my two oldest children or their mother. That would end on a winter day in 2005. I was walking into a local mall and held the door for a woman and her children who were exiting, when I made eye contact with the woman. I immediately looked beyond her to lock my eyes on the boy and girl that walked behind her. As soon as her eyes met mine it was like I was looking in a mirror, and as I looked at him I knew that I was looking at my children. Emotion was running high but I knew I had to be calm and not scare them or create a scene. Holly indicated that the child support agency had been looking for me.

Emotion was running high but I knew I had to be calm and not scare them or create a scene. Holly indicated that the child support agency had been looking for me so that I could begin to pay child support. Her first words after all those years and my attempts to connect were about child support. I was momentarily speechless. I acknowledged the kids who were standing at their mother's side with looks on their faces that read, "Who the hell is this?" I provided Holly with my contact information and indicated that I'd be reaching out to the folks at the child support enforcement agency first thing in the morning. At this point I was newly married, and now I had the task of going home and explaining this entire situation that began in 1993 to my wife. I knew the conversation wouldn't go over too well.

I shared early on during our courtship that there were two children that I had fathered but had been pushed away from them by their mother because of my actions as a teenager, but there had never been any conversations since then. I was now about to walk into our home and tell her that not only had I encountered them for the first time in my adult life, but I was also about to be paying child support--taking money out of our home when I was hardly making any.

As I entered the house I rushed up stairs to find her lying in bed. She could tell by my expression that there was something on my mind and my heart. As I shared what had just happened, she began to cry. That same day, she had found out from her doctor that she was expecting our first child, and couldn't wait for me to get home to share the news. My news sucked the life out of her being able to tell me that we were expecting. I was filled with so many emotions. I had gone from a father of none, to a father of three in a matter of hours. That night didn't go well at all in our home, and it would forever set the tone for our home life and marriage.

I kept my word and made it my first priority that next morning to reach out and make sure I was accessible for whatever process may come from the child support agency. The first step was to establish paternity. I showed up ready to take the DNA test and to my surprise, both of my children were sitting there quietly. At the time, they were 12 and 13-years-old. I had no idea where to start, what to say, or how to act. Before I could even begin with a hello, our names were called. The experience will forever be embedded in my memory because I felt so bad for them having to sit through something that no child should ever have to sit through. And yet, here they were with their mother and father, but it would take a stranger with some cotton swabs to tell them what I already knew for sure.

I was their father. Soon after the results were official, a support order was established and I began to contribute financially, but that wasn't enough for me. I attempted to reach out to Holly again because I had a million questions I wanted to ask. The predominant one being: why now after all of these years? She always knew how to contact me, even while I was in college. I also wanted to know if the years had changed her heart and she was at a place where she could now support my efforts to connect with my children and build a relationship. Those questions, along with many others, were never answered by way of an adult conversation.

I was determined to build a relationship with them with or without her support. The challenge for me was twofold: I was trying to connect with my children after thirteen years of absence, and I was trying to grow my recent marriage and prepare for my first child with my wife. Holly didn't do much in my opinion by way of encouraging the kids to reciprocate my attempts at communicating. I would attempt to get to know them by having conversations about school, friends, their interests, and home life. Honestly, the first few conversations were very awkward because I didn't know where to begin.

It was noticeable that it was awkward for them as well to be on the phone basically with a stranger. Over the course of the next few months, the phone calls on both sides would decrease, and it was evident that there wasn't much of an interest on their part. There were also a couple of times we planned to meet at pubic locations, and I would have to cancel due to drama at home or my wife and daughter needing me. Canceling on them disappointed them, and it made it seem as if I was not really serious about building any relationship with them. They grew to not trust me with my word, and that lack of trust prohibited them from wanting anything to do with me. It was such a frustrating position to be in. The anger and frustration from my son could be seen in the emails that he would send me basically telling me that he thought that I was a loser, and he wanted nothing to do with me at all.

I've been fortunate to be afforded the opportunity to spend some time with my oldest daughter, although the time has often been very little. She has been willing to communicate and see me and allow us an opportunity to get to know each other. A few years passed with me still married with two children with my wife, when one day I invited her over to my house for a cookout.

It was to be the first time she would see her sister and brother, and also the first time my wife would have any interaction with her. I was so excited about the day as it presented a first step in what I had always wanted. However, the day would end in disaster. My wife's actions and demeanor with the arrival of my daughter was nothing short of unwelcoming. The lack of communication and the distance during the visit was clear not only to me, but to my daughter. And although my two youngest kids enjoyed the time spent with her, they were not really able to conceptualize what was taking place, and my daughter made it very clear that she would never return again.

I never truly felt any support from my wife in developing that relationship with the two oldest kids. And even though her actions from that day were not intentional, especially considering she asked not be present in the first place, the damage was already done. Any discussions around them were sometimes met with slight resistance. I felt a sense of loyalty to what I had at home with my two younger kids, and so I never truly put as much effort into reaching out as I should have. As the oldest grew, time began to be drastically shorter, and any efforts to connect with my son were met with his verbal aggression and anger. Even though he doesn't acknowledge me as his father, I am sure to acknowledge him.

Over the years following my divorce, I've extended an open invitation for him and I to connect, meet, and have a conversation to attempt to build a relationship. During conversations with him via social networking sites, he has made it clear that he doesn't acknowledge me as his father and addresses me by my first name. His words have drawn me to tears many times, as he has made it clear that he has no intentions of culivating a relationship with me, stating that I blew that chance years ago. In the absence of being able to spend time with him I learned that he was an athlete, and I was sure to go and watch him perform from afar. I was respectful of his wishes, so I kept my distance and never attempted to be seen or speak to him. With the both of them in high school by this time, all of the communication came by way of social networking and texting.

171

Although I had very little to do with her success, I was delighted and blessed to have been present for my oldest daughter's high school graduation and watch her move on to college. I 257 During conversations with him via social networking sites, he has made it clear that he doesn't acknowledge me as his father and addresses me by my first name. His words have drawn me to tears many times, as he has made it clear that he has no intentions of wanting to have a relationship with me, stating that I blew that chance years ago. In the absence of being able to spend time with him I learned that he was an athlete, and I was sure to go and watch him perform from afar.

I was respectful of his wishes, so I kept my distance and never attempted to be seen or speak to him while I was there. With the both of them in high school by this time, all of the communication came by way of social networking and texting. Although I had very little to do with her success, I was delighted and blessed to have been present for my oldest daughter's high school graduation and watch her move on to college. I still reach out to the both of them via phone or Facebook. I still offer anything that I can to help them, but the offer is never accepted. Essentially, I have watched them grow and know more about them from social media sites than actual physical interaction.

They are both adults now, and I always pray that one day they will forgive me and not judge me on my past, but instead look at who I am now and want what I've always wanted: a relationship with them. It had been very difficult for me to finish writing this chapter, and for months it was never completed. There were nights that I became very frustrated and no matter how hard I tried to complete this chapter, it just wouldn't work. So I would move on to another chapter for completion and return to this one. But I knew why it was difficult and God continued to talk to me, telling me what I needed to do.

One of the things that I've realized in my journey while impacting the lives of others is that God will not move you to truly do HIS work if you're not honest with yourself. Although I knew what God was telling me, I continued to write other chapters. One day while on Facebook, I received a private message that read, "Hey this is Amy! Hopefully you remember me. Please contact me, your son really needs you." As I read the message, tears began to flow down my face, and I was filled with so much emotion.

As I read the message, tears began to flow down my face, and I was filled with so much emotion. Years of living in denial and selective forgetfulness had gone by, but the Facebook message I received from Amy pulled all that I am and had become into instant accountability.

I was finally at a place where I could acknowledge that I fathered a son while I was living in a foster home, before any of my other children were even possibilities. I asked God to open my heart and my mind to the possibilities. Over the years, I had secretly attempted to search for his mother, but never really put enough effort into it to be successful. I responded to the private message and began communicating with the mother. I knew exactly who she was, and I was prepared to face reality. At the time she told me that my son was named Cameron. He was 20-years-old, and for some time now had been asking for and about me.

She told me that they had moved from Ohio to Virginia, which was the main reason I couldn't locate her. As I read down the screen to continue learning about my 20-year-old son on Facebook, nothing could have prepared me for what I was about to read. I asked for his whereabouts because if he needed me, I was prepared to be wherever he was. She shared that he was in a Virginia jail awaiting sentencing on federal charges, facing three to four years in prison. My heart suddenly resided where my stomach used to be, and I stood in disbelief.

It was my fault I told myself as I cried. I hadn't been there for him and didn't have an opportunity to take responsibility. Without hesitation, I provided Amy with my contact information so that he and I could connect. In just a few weeks after my initial contact with Amy, while I was having dinner with a friend I received a phone call. Initially, I looked at my phone and didn't recognize the number, so I sent the call to voicemail.

The phone rang again from the same number and I hesitantly answered the phone. Before I had an opportunity to say hello the caller said, "Hey, is this Rayshawn?" "Yes, and who is this?" I replied. "Hey Dad, how you doing? It's Cameron." With great excitement and an equal amount of nervousness, I replied to him, but I didn't answer his question. Prior to my phone call with him, I spent hours in deep thought wondering what I would say to him when finally given the chance. I'm never at a loss for words, but even while trying to have the conversation in my fantasy, the words never came to me.

Once it registered that he had just called me "Dad", and that his voice indicated that he was excited to be on the phone with me for the first time in either of our lives, my mouth was silenced and my heart spoke. "Cameron, I'm sorry. I'm sorry for not being there for you. I'm sorry for not taking responsibility like I should have years ago, and I hope that you can find it in your heart to forgive me." His response was in line with the excitement I felt from his greeting: "Man, Dad you don't know how good it feels to finally hear your voice. I already forgave you a long time ago, and now I just want to move forward and build a relationship with you."

I was overcome with a joy that I could have never imagined. The timing was definitely divine intervention because it was shortly after I had finished my initial draft of this very chapter, and the fact that I'd been discussing forgiveness and accountability was more confirmation that God was moving mountains so that I could be the kind of father that I wanted to be. Over the next five minutes we went back and forth exchanging information about each other, and despite the interruptions from the automated message in the background that states the time remaining on the call, we made the best of our first conversation. Before hanging up the phone, I made a promise to Cameron that although I had not been around for his first twenty years, that I was here now to support him in any way I could, and to do everything possible to be a father to him.

The phone call ended with such a huge burden being lifted from my shoulders, and although he is in prison, I felt a connection that I know would continue to grow. I received a letter from him shortly after that phone call the following week.

Hey Dad,

I just got off the phone with you, and the first thing I want to say is I'm extremely happy to have you in my life. I can't begin to tell you how great of a feeling this is for me right now. My social worker found my mom for me when I was seventeen. She was in jail , so I never really took the time to build a relationship with her. Man I really feel complete in my life. Your testimony about making it in the same system that I'm trying to fight my way out of is really inspiring. It's actually euphoric, and it gives me a substantial amount of hope while I'm confined within these walls. That's cool that you played college football. At some point I swore I was going to make it in sports because I had excelled in them, but I guess God had a different path for me. I still enjoy playing them and I keep up with them professionally. My favorite teams are the Falcons, the Cleveland Cavaliers, and Ohio State. Music is my remedy. I am a very good artist and I actually have many people out here waiting for a new project. I write Hip-Hop and R &B songs, and I'm not trying to sound cocky when I say that I have perfected my craft. My style is so different, and I rap about my past struggles, my relationships with women, and that kind of stuff. I have a song on YouTube recorded four years ago called "Help" by Spayce. That's what everyone calls me, it's pronounced Space. Anyway, check it out when you can! It's old and I've come a long way since that recording. I do plan on getting out and attempting to record at least two mixtapes and an album, and I'm excited to bring my sound to the Midwest. I can't wait to get out in 2016, if not sooner, Lord willing. I can't say that my life has been normal. I was adopted at age eleven by a nice couple, but I knew in my heart that wasn't the right place for me.

I got into trouble, stole things, and I fought them and anybody else. Overall, I've been homeless numerous times, spent time in group homes, and I ended up going to four different high schools. School was never really hard for me; I just got so tired of being moved around that I focused my attention on surviving. So I ended up dropping out to focus on hustling, girls, and partying. I eventually got my GED, which came so easy for me I passed it on my first try. Math is and always has been very difficult for me, but I didn't let it stop me. When I wasn't homeless, I lived with girls, got small jobs to pay the bills but things went bad one year, and I lost everything. I started to break into houses and do whatever I needed in order to get by. Things soon caught up with me from stealing, and that's why I'm faced with this time. So here I am now seeking redemption and forgiveness for all I've done and looking for a support system. Being united with you is significant because I actually feel like I have something to come home to. I am without a doubt coming back to Ohio upon my release, and please understand Dad that I want nothing to do with a life of crime anymore. I'm really not a bad person and I'm positive that I can get out here and make something of my life. I do fear though that I won't fit into your world. You have four other kids so right now it's hard for me to picture how I will fit in. It's overwhelming to hear that I have siblings who are doing so well and that I was born on the same day just a different year as my oldest sister on August 4th! I hope when it's all said and done that they don't reject me as a brother. I have always felt out of place my entire life without you and I just want to be your son. I have intentions of going to college for either graphic design or journalism. Anyway, it was so good to talk to you Dad and know that I love you and I'm looking forward to building a relationship with you.

Peace & One Love,

Your oldest Boy

Over the next several months after getting that letter and knowing more about him, I felt as if I was looking at myself and giving myself advice. I learned that even though we had different paths, we shared the same struggles and listening to him I learned that he's wanted something that I always wanted: to know and have a relationship with his dad. If I could send the clock in reverse I would do anything within my power to regain the opportunity to be a better father to my children. Even if it meant that I made mistakes along the way and had to learn while I was doing it, I'm sure it would have been better for them and me because I still would have been there.

Reading his letter I felt as if I was reading about myself all over again. Reading his letter and having the conversations that I've had with him, I hear a hunger in his voice and passion from his words that indicate his desire to be a better man. In such a short period we learned that we have so much in common, but the one commonality that stands out is his determination and courage. He's made it clear that he wants a better life.

I remember that feeling and I also know how it felt to have that feeling, but no support system in place to help achieve it. I look forward to being that for him. Who he is will ensure that he'll be able to endure. Who I've become will ensure he doesn't do it alone. Whether learning to ride a bike, or navigating difficult life situations, I've learned that is the true essence of fatherhood.

Who'd think in elementary? Heeey! I see the penitentiary, one day And runnin from the police, that's right Mama catch me, put a whoopin to my backside And even as a crack fiend, mama You always was a black queen, mama I finally understand for a woman it ain't easy tryin to raise a man You always was committed A poor single mother on welfare, tell me how ya did it? There's no way I can pay you back But the plan is to show you that I understand You are appreciated. Dear Mama,

~Tupac, Dear Mama

DEAR MAMA

Dear Mama,

I'll start this letter off by simply saying Mama, I love you. Death often robs us of the ability to express our love, and leaves survivors of turbulent pasts full of regret. Since your death in 2006, I have carried words in my heart meant for your ears that will never quite find their home. There are so many conversations I wish that we could have had before you left. The sense of abandonment I felt while growing up, and knowing that my childhood was full of things that no child should have to encounter caused a lot of resentment. Depending on the day of the week, or the prevailing emotion, my thoughts about our relationship tend to be as random as pulling numbers from a hat. I hate that your addiction affected me the way it did. That disease was the reason I was pin-balled from several group homes and foster homes, which also led to me attending three different elementary schools, four middle schools, and four high schools. The only things that were certain for Jamil and I was that we never knew where we'd have to call home next, and that even when we were in your care, it wouldn't be long before we were gone again. Before my formal education, I hated that you chose drugs and men over us. I still feel like I was robbed of my childhood, and like I was an unwanted burden. I didn't ask to be conceived, nor did I ask to live a life of luxury and fame. I would have settled for a little of what I

178

considered to be normal, but instead there aren't too many memories of my life as a child that felt or even feel normal today. I have no idea why we left California when I was young, but I do remember the day you told me to give my dad a hug and a kiss goodbye. I remember holding on to his neck tightly and not wanting to let go. That hug and kiss would be the last contact and only memory I would ever have of my father. There have been times in my life when I wish that I could return to that moment and stay in his embrace. Instead, you pulled me from his arms and out of his life to move clear across the map. And for what, to live inthe projects? For so long I have felt like I was begging you to love me. I remember trying to find ways to be noticed so you would give me your attention, and at times settling for negative attention as opposed to no attention at all. Getting into trouble and mischief seemed to work the best, but I know now that it only worked because it had the potential to affect your life. I was terrified during those lonely nights when you would leave me to look after Jamil while you partied and gave your time and energy to the streets. I wasn't equipped to make adult decisions, so I made them based on what allowed me to eat, have fun, or stay safe. Looking back, having to steal in order to quiet the stomach rumblings from hunger should have been the last thing on my young mind. But not only were the thoughts on my mind, those thoughts became my actions. The fact that you missed so many key moments in my life made them all feel incomplete, like they didn't matter as much and would have been more meaningful if you were there. Getting up from being tackled on the football field and being able to look to my mom in the stands to let her know I'm okay wasn't a part of my athletic experience. Pictures with you after earning my college and graduate degrees don't sit in frames on my mantle. There was no mother of the groom to be led down the aisle at my wedding. My children will never hear grandma say, "You look just like your daddy when he was little," and it all hurts so much. The accumulation of pain from all of those harsh realities caused hurt to turn to resentment, and finally hatred. For years, I carried that around not for you, but for my experience. The more I internalized what I

had been through and how life was a series of events that were mainly out of my control, the more I began to feel like I had been a victim. Since I felt like a victim, it seemed the most logical thing to do from that point was to play the role. I blamed you for many of my own mistakes, including my two years in prison. Everything that went or was going wrong I could look to my childhood and lack of parental stability as a contributing factor. I've had many sleepless nights crying over thoughts of you, and because of that pain, it was hard for me to let go of my past in order to move on to live the life that I was capable of living. My feelings toward you were manifested in my relationships with women and were a factor in why it was so easy for me to objectify, use, and ultimately hurt them. On the other side of all the fear, uncertainty, and moments where I felt like we were not important were the times when I could see that you were doing the very best you could. I appreciate the times when you worked two nursing jobs to make sure we had a roof over our heads and food on the table, even if it wasn't the things children like to eat. Seeing you work like that instilled a very tenacious work ethic in me, and that's one of the things that still serve me very well. Regardless of the
pain or level of suffering I endured, I can still hear you say to me, "Son, no matter what, don't you ever give up fighting for what you want and believe in." Those words have been on repeat in the soundtrack of my life and when life has been at its most chaotic state, I can hear you whisper those words in my ear. Hearing those words has given me the courage, motivation, and determination to keep fighting, even when I think all hope has been lost. Being able to grow, mature and develop has brought about a lot of change in my life. Additionally, fatherhood did something to me that I wish I could bottle and sell to every man. I was suddenly able to understand what it means to love someone without conditions, and to be committed to being there for them no matter what may come. I have also been able to discover what it feels like when a man forgives and is forgiven. Mama, I'm happy to say that I no longer harbor feelings of resentment towards you and hate for my life's circumstances. Actually, I love you more now than I ever

have before. I learned to appreciate you and what you stood for, and because I forgive you, I'm now fully able to let go and move on to a much healthier life. Letting go of the anger, hurt, and the baggage that was weighing me down over the past several years has been life changing. Holding on to those things would have had me stuck, and I have been able to break free and pursue my breakthrough. Still, not too many days go by that don't bring a thought of you. I find myself being able to recall fond memories and reasons to smile when I think of you. I truly miss those times. On your birthdays, instead of crying over your death, I celebrate you by sharing messages of addiction and recovery to honor your life, and in hopes of saving someone else's. Every opportunity I have to get in front of people and educate them about addiction puts you in front of the room sharing your story. I feel you in my spirit because when I'm there, so are you. Every time I have a meal that consists of fried chicken, homemade macaroni and cheese, greens seasoned with smoked turkey, and cornbread, I'm reminded of what a great cook you were. Your favorite Sunday meal is also mine, and when I'm lucky enough to have a meal that reminds me of your cooking, it feeds my soul. Even though I'm not a Muslim as you were, I still continue to honor you by not eating pork, and the times when I have by mistake, I still get sick to my stomach. So I thank you for the gentle reminder. I'm regularly reminded of the struggles I experienced growing up, but they've made me appreciate so many things in life. I couldn't see it while I was in it but as an adult it's crystal clear. I'm reminded about how confused I used to be on why you insisted that I save the small pieces of bath soap and place them in a bag, until the days came when we didn't have any soap to wash, or when we didn't have dishwashing detergent and you would make me boil those soap bars and use it to wash the dishes. From those pieces of soap, I learned to be resourceful. The times you made me stand in those long food pantry lines to sign us up for free food items were some of my least favorite times, but the days came when we didn't have any food and because we signed up early, all we had to do was go pick up the boxes. From those food boxes, I learned to be forward-thinking and frugal.

Because of these and many other experiences, I now understand and appreciate so much because of those trying times. When I think back, all of the struggles resulted in learning experiences. Those childhood experiences continue to be packed full of lessons that teach me even now as an adult. Innovation is key to survival, and I'm blessed to have had so many experiences that help me survive on a daily basis. I never understood why God took you from me so soon and before you could get out of prison so we could redevelop that relationship that we both talked about. It would've been nice to share these words with you in person, but even though you're not here with me physically, your spirit lives within me. It was so hard for me for so many years to say these three words to you for many reasons, but now that I'm free from the hurt and pain, I don't want another day to go by without saying that I love you. Through the letters we exchanged and prison visits, I began to notice the change in your attitude and outlook on life. I noticed your desire to create a better life for yourself after prison and addiction. Your will and determination lives within me and every time I think about quitting, I can see your face. When I think about what you were going to do with your life, it feels like I've been watching a DVD that freezes just as the movie is getting to the good part. The sad part is despite your best efforts, you fought your addiction the best you could until your very last breath. Mama, while you're reading this, please try not to cry. I will write again soon. Until then, please know that I keep you in my heart, my prayers, and my thoughts. The best is yet to come and as I bring this letter to a close I'll end it the same way I started it:

Mama, I love you.

Your son, Rayshawn

"Life is only a reflection of what we allow ourselves to see."
~Unknown

THE ROAR OF TRUTH

Racism feeds many people's souls in this country. Sadly, so many have not lost their appetite and still sneak portions while no one is watching, while others turn the other way as if they don't see what is taking place. That racism is evident in our criminal justice system in which so many minorities are disproportionately represented in prisons all across the country, particularly in private prisons where major corporations are profiting billions and billions of dollars. Companies such as The GEO Group, Inc. and CCA, the two largest private for-profit prisons, spend millions of dollars lobbying for harsh sentences that would put more people in jail.

Once passed into a bill, those harsh sentences largely impact the African-American community. Numbers don't lie and the facts beg the question: is this by chance or circumstance? However, we can no longer use race as an excuse for not getting ahead. Even though racism is still a part of economic and social systems, policies, and laws in this country, it is my opinion that we as African- Americans hurt ourselves and do just as much damage in our own communities as those racist systems and policies. I have always been told that life is 90% attitude and 10% how we react to it. Many of us leave the prison and solely focus on the harm that has been done to us, instead of coming away from the experience with purpose and a plan for reaching our goals.

Even if you are moving in the right direction, you will never reach your destination or full potential with the wrong attitude. In other words, a bad attitude will surely hinder your progress and block the many blessings that God has intended for you. Success can no longer only be defined by staying out of prison once released. In direct contradiction to the philosophy that we should create a name for ourselves, many of us who have been involved in the criminal justice system allow the terms to define who we were, and who we will be. The objective should be to move as far away from those negative terms in every way possible, especially in our actions, our daily lives, and in our mentality.

Learning from the past and acknowledging it does not mean that the past dictates the future. Yes, you may have come from some very difficult circumstances, but the question that you have to ask yourself is, "How will I be the master of my fate and the captain of my soul?" Most people that know my story are more interested in what I am doing today. Very seldom do people want to know about the past, primarily because regardless of what happened, there is nothing that can be done about it. Many times we live so much in the past that it keeps us from moving ahead and receiving the other blessings that God has in store for us.

If you are reading this from behind bars, please know that I understand your struggles and pain, but I want you to understand that only you can make a change in your life. If you do not have the desire to change for yourself, there is nothing a correctional officer, the institution, a doctor, parole officer, or psychologist will be able to do for you. It takes a combination of resilience, ambition, perseverance, and most importantly faith in a higher power, to beat the odds and the criminal justice system. Everyone has it within himself or herself; it's just a matter of tapping into that source. Being open to the possibilities, soul searching, and forming a relationship with the creator is the place to begin.

Over 600,000 ex-offenders are released each year, 1,600 per day are from correctional institutions. This means that hitting the streets with a hustler's mentality puts you a day behind yesterday's free man who already beat you to the crumbs that you'll fight over. New and improved hustles only guarantee you a one-way ticket back to the "cell motel." Please understand that despite what you may have been taught out there in the streets or through the media, the streets don't love you. It just takes you away from the people that really do. Being locked up and caged can no longer be a rite of passage or badge of honor for our boys and young men. There are enough things working against us when we steer clear of legal troubles.

Finally, the impact of incarceration will always be perceived as insurmountable in the Black community if we don't get back to having and instilling family values in our households. Parents not accepting and taking responsibility for raising our children is part of the reason we are at this crucial point in our existence. It's not enough for parents to expect children to do as they say, for children are always watching more of what we do and learn to model those behaviors as such. Social service agencies are not parents; they are created so that the majority of the population doesn't have to feel the effect of so many of us not having access to equal economics. If you were recently released, regardless of how long you were down, the realest aspect of "doing time" begins now.

This is the time period where you're going be tested to see where your heart really is, especially if you're black, and how you really want it. The world will not care if you are trying to do whatever you identify as the right thing. You are going to get overlooked for multiple jobs, denied housing, denied public benefits, and looked at like rehabilitation is not possible. You will even be seen as less of a person. How society views and treats us should not be the way we view and treat ourselves. Don't be ashamed of who you are, where you have come from, and most importantly, what you are about to become. It is because of the things that happened in the past that you are where and who you are today. In truth, none of us can truly let go of the past until we have faced it and understood it, and that requires not just private consideration, but also action.

Our past haunts us until we look at it squarely and allow it to teach us how and how not to live as we move on. Stand tall, be proud yet humble, and continue to move forward with a sense of purpose. When the opportunity arises reach back to those who are where you once found yourself. Once you find yourself giving back, others will do the same by paying it forward. Attitude makes the difference between the people who succeed or fail in life after going through trying times. You can be pitiful or you can be powerful during those times, but you can't be both.

So today, right now, while going through a difficult time, you have to choose. Yes change is hard, trust me I understand that, but you can suffer the pain of change and endure, or suffer in remaining the way you are. In some cases choosing the latter could be the equivalent of a life sentence in prison or even worse, death. The excuses you may be using today are the same ones that are holding you back from living a better life for tomorrow. Excuses are thinking errors that give us this false sense of security by telling you it's okay to continue with negative behavior or continue to be content with where you are at in life. I made up my mind a long time ago that in all areas of my life, I would refuse to settle for anything less than what I knew I deserved.

Settling means you don't believe that you are worth something better. The moment I stopped playing the victim and making excuses, things started to change in every aspect of my life. I decided that I would live my life by design and not by default, meaning that I would be more in control and not let other things or people control my destiny. You can't be so anxious to improve your circumstances, but unwilling to invest to improve yourself. You take you wherever you go, meaning you may move away from the circumstances, but you are still bound by your thought processes. At the heart of transformation in every person is their thought processes.

In order for change to take place in areas of our lives in which we are struggling and being held hostage, we must examine our attitudes, values, and beliefs--things that cannot be seen that are deeply rooted inside of us, which ultimately have an impact on our behavior. A person is literally what he thinks, his character being the complete sum of all of his thoughts. As the plant springs forth from the seed, so every act of a man springs forth from the hidden seeds of thought, and could not have appeared without them. Our actions then are the blossoms of our thoughts, and joy and suffering are its fruit. When we are honest with ourselves and willing to dig deep into our souls, only then is when treasure of truth is found.

Good thoughts and actions can never produce bad results, just as bad thoughts and actions can never produce good results. When individuals are suffering from consequences, it is always the effect of negative thinking in some capacity. It is an indication that the individual is out of harmony with himself, and must find ways to gain balance, or continue to suffer. Often times we don't directly choose our circumstances but we can choose our thoughts, and therefore surely shape our circumstances. Our thoughts are directly connected to our purpose, and if your thoughts are not linked with purpose, there is no true accomplishment.

Just like a physically weak man can make himself strong by careful and patient training, so can a person of negative weak thinking make themselves strong and positive by exercising righteous thinking. It is my sincere desire for each reader to see a personal characteristic and adopt a different one because when God created me, He put the heart of a lion in my chest which through each beat, helped me to develop the ambition, perseverance, fortitude, resilience, and faith necessary to take charge of my own life and direct my own future. Once my soul searching was complete, I knew it was there and I embraced it. Each day I rise with a sense of purpose and renewed faith, and I am no different from anyone else who does the same. It is not only just in me, it is in all of us; we just have to be willing to seize the moment. Thank you for reading, and may your LionHeart guide and serve you well on your journey as you continue to Rise & Roar!

Rayshawn "The LionHeart" Wilson

Made in the USA
Lexington, KY
21 September 2017